James Joyce

Very Interesting People

Bite-sized biographies of Britain's most fascinating historical figures

James Joyce

Very Interesting **VIP** *People*

Bruce Stewart

OXFORD
UNIVERSITY PRESS

OXFORD
UNIVERSITY PRESS

Great Clarendon Street, Oxford ox2 6DP

Oxford University Press is a department of the University of Oxford.
It furthers the University's objective of excellence in research, scholarship,
and education by publishing worldwide in

Oxford New York

Auckland Cape Town Dar es Salaam Hong Kong Karachi
Kuala Lumpur Madrid Melbourne Mexico City Nairobi
New Delhi Shanghai Taipei Toronto

With offices in

Argentina Austria Brazil Chile Czech Republic France Greece
Guatemala Hungary Italy Japan Poland Portugal Singapore
South Korea Switzerland Thailand Turkey Ukraine Vietnam

Oxford is a registered trade mark of Oxford University Press
in the UK and in certain other countries

Published in the United States
by Oxford University Press Inc., New York

First published in the *Oxford Dictionary of National Biography* 2004
This paperback edition first published 2007

British Library Cataloguing in Publication Data

Data available

Library of Congress Cataloging in Publication Data

Data available

Typeset by SPI Publisher Services, Pondicherry, India
Printed in Great Britain
on acid-free paper by
Ashford Colour Press Ltd, Gosport, Hampshire

ISBN 978–0–19–921752–6 (Pbk.)

10 9 8 7 6 5 4 3 2 1

Contents

Preface

In writing a commissioned article on James Joyce for the *Oxford Dictionary of National Biography* (2004)—from which this brief life stems—I was inevitably driven to enquire how far that writer was a proper candidate for inclusion in a 'national' biography with its feet securely planted on English *terra firma*. Certainly he is an indispensable presence in any Irish national dictionary of the kind. Does inclusion in one imply exclusion from the other? The editors of the British compilation have a clear prerogative in relation to this question: it is their dictionary after all. Furthermore, it is their language, in so far as Joyce can justly be said to have written in English despite the polyglottal tendencies of his last creation.

As one who was born within hailing distance of most addresses at which Joyce lived in Ireland

and who inherits the same social and cultural experience (albeit at an earlier historical stage), it involves for me a perceptible effort to put aside the conviction that, since the study of Irish literature in English set up in earnest during the 1970s, Joyce has been assimilated more or less completely to the Irish cultural corpus. This, of course, is false: while Joyce's distinctive sensibility and genius can be said to spring from Irish conditions his ultimate resting-place is surely within the English pale and—albeit in a problematic way—he thus assumes a place of great distinction in the English literary tradition. This remains true notwithstanding his own attachment to continental writers and his recent co-option by Francophone philosophers of the post-structuralist movement.

The 'Englishness' of Irish writers is nothing new. As the *Oxford DNB* editors well know, many are virtually immune to the form of sequestration that arises from Irish separatist designs (for example, Congreve, Swift, Sheridan, Wilde). All such writers are, properly speaking, exponents of English literature in Ireland and quite rightly known as 'Anglo-Irish'—a pseudo-ethnological literary tradition that includes such late blooms as

Elizabeth Bowen and Molly Keane. (Others, such as Aidan Higgins, Jennifer Johnston, and John Banville, slip in by virtue of their exploitation of the genre.) By contrast, few men and women writing in Ireland today are claimed for English literature, or only at the price of occasionally ruffled feathers as in the case of Seamus Heaney. In some respects, therefore, the Irish sea has become a greater barrier in proportion as the distance between Dublin and Paris or Brussels (and all the world besides) becomes shorter.

All of this is perhaps a function of the devolutionary tendency without British culture no less than the powerful agency of Irish nation-building or the emergence of the Celtic Tiger. The fact remains, however, that James Joyce turned his face against nationalism in the form in which it presented itself to him as a young man in Ireland; and when, in March 1922, the Irish foreign minister Desmond Fitzgerald offered him a passport, he refused it. *Ipso facto*, he is a British writer so far as the diplomatic corps is concerned; and, if only for that reason I have no qualms about his inclusion in the British dictionary and my own small part as a literary undertaker.

Any new 'life' of Joyce necessarily bears witness to the monumental scale of Richard Ellmann's research and writing in *James Joyce* (1959; rev. edn. 1982). The amount of new information discovered since makes little difference to the tale as told by him. Hence the schedule of places, events and publications set out in this biographical essay broadly follows the pattern established by him. I have differed only in little ways—as, for instance, in accepting with Peter Costello (1992) that E. C. in *A Portrait of the Artist as a Young Man* was not a Sheehy but another student at the Royal University, and in placing the 'Christmas Dinner' episode in that novel in Blackrock and not in Bray on the basis of my own familiarity with the houses in question.

These and other details are externalities. What was going on inside the mind—the lived experience of James Joyce—is of course much harder to capture in a biographical article though this is just what the greatest biographers actually do. It generally falls to critics to attempt it since every interpretation of the works is necessarily in some degree an assertion about the mental and emotional processes in which it is founded (conscious or unconscious, semiological or metaphysical). In reviewing that literature I have been constantly struck by the regularity with which Joyce has been hijacked for ideological purposes quite remote from his own imaginative processes. If an Irish postcolonial context promises the best hope of explaining his extraordinary development as an experimental author (as I argue here), there are still aesthetic and epistemological traces to be found in his earliest writings—and especially in the notebook materials which have just resurfaced and have been secured by the National Library of Ireland—which suggest a fixity of design which modern literary-critical approaches tend to over-look or, what is worse, to dismiss for their own rea-sons. It seems to me, for instance, that the aesthetic ideas which Joyce cogged from Aristotle as a young man are of much greater significance at every stage of his career than has been thought. It seems to me that his adherence to the idea of the 'word incarnate' in all its phenomenological complexity has more to do with the principles of innovation in his art than anyone has yet considered. It is in this spirit that I say that a truly Joycean interpretation of Joyce's literary development has not perhaps yet been seen. I hope that, without eccentricity, I can bring it forward in the future.

Bruce Stewart
February 2007

About the author

Bruce Stewart lectures in Irish literary history and bibliography at the University of Ulster. He has taught in Ireland and the Middle East as well as Britain and America and has contributed widely to Irish-studies journals. For many years he was secretary of the International Association for the Studies of Irish Literatures, and has also served as Literary Director of the Princess Grace Irish Library in Monaco. He is currently completing a critical monograph on Joyce. His Irish upbringing was in many respects like Joyce's, with whom he shares a birthday.

Destined to be elusive

1

James Augustine Aloysius Joyce (1882–1941), writer, was born at 41 Brighton Square, West Rathgar, Dublin, on 2 February 1882, the eldest surviving son of John Stanislaus Joyce (1849–1931) and his wife, Mary Jane (May) (1859–1903), daughter of John Murray and Margaret Theresa Murray. The Joyces were a Catholic middle-class family who had enjoyed moderate commercial prosperity in Cork and Dublin throughout the nineteenth century. The family was aligned on both sides with constitutional nationalism, although the Joyces were the more substantial property-owners and the more socially secure representatives of the emerging Catholic bourgeoisie. They boasted a connection with Daniel O'Connell through Joyce's paternal grandmother. Purportedly descended

from Thomas de Jorce, John Stanislaus laid somewhat specious claim to a heraldic coat of arms
bearing the legend *Pernobilis et pervetusta familia*
('Most famous and ancient family').

Parents and family

Joyce called his father 'the silliest man I ever
knew', but he also attributed to him his own 'good
tenor voice, and an extravagant licentious dispo-
sition' (Ellmann, *Joyce*, 643). John Joyce is the
model for Simon Dedalus in *A Portrait of the
Artist as a Young Man* (1916) and *Ulysses* (1922),
and—somewhat more diffusely—the model for
Earwicker in *Finnegans Wake* (1939). He plays a
larger role than any other relative in an *œuvre*
which T. S. Eliot later found so pervasively autobiographical. Interest in Joyce's family background
seems 'not only suggested by our own inquisi-
tiveness, but almost expected by [Joyce] himself'
(preface to S. Joyce, *My Brother's Keeper*, 11–12).
Throughout his life James Joyce tirelessly revis-
ited his own family history as well as the wider life
of the city in which he was born, transforming the
'sluggish matter' of experience into the 'imper-
ishable' substance of art—as his autobiographical

alter ego Stephen Dedalus pronounces in the *Portrait*.

John Stanislaus Joyce was born on 4 July 1849. After a short time at school, and to improve his health, he was sent out on pilot ships of the transatlantic steamers from Queenstown (Cobh), which coloured his vocabulary in ways he transmitted to the next generation. His taste for operatic music also greatly influenced the novelist's sensibility. He became active in Fenian politics before moving in the mid-1870s to Dublin, where he sang in public and private to such effect that he earned the name 'a successor to Campanini'. He also sang in the company of Barton M'Guckin at the Antient Concert Rooms—a distinction echoed by his son when he sang at the same venue in company with John McCormack some thirty years later.

At the end of the 1870s John Stanislaus entered into partnership with one Henry Alleyn in the Dublin and Chapelizod Distillery but lost his £500 investment when Alleyn embezzled the company's funds (an injury that James Joyce avenged in naming the disagreeable solicitor in 'Counterparts' after him). In 1880 he became collector of rates for Inns Quay and Rotunda wards, a reward for services to the United Liberal Club. On 5 May 1880 he married May Murray, ten years his junior. She was the daughter of an agent for wines and spirits from co. Longford—a family background that John Stanislaus Joyce considered inferior to his own and often disparaged: 'O weeping God, the things I married into' (*Ulysses*, 47). They married against the wishes of both their parents, and John Stanislaus's mother never forgave him for it. But May was brought up well enough to have been a fellow pupil of Katharine Tynan at Misses Flynn School, where dancing, *politesse*, and the piano were taught (providing the setting for 'The Dead'), and May's sister-in-law Josephine (*née* Giltrap) was the older relative for whom Joyce had the most respectful, good-humoured, and affectionate regard throughout his life.

John Stanislaus and May Joyce settled at 47 Northumberland Avenue, Kingstown (now Dun Laoghaire). A first child, John Augustine Joyce, was born in 1881 but did not survive. In December of that year John Stanislaus took out the first of a succession of mortgages which marked his economic decline in future years.

James, the first surviving child, was baptized at St Joseph's Chapel of Ease, Roundtown, Dublin (now St Joseph's Church, Terenure), on 5 February 1882, when he was erroneously registered as James Augusta Joyce. In the ensuing twelve years, May Joyce endured thirteen more pregnancies, bearing four boys and six girls, with three miscarriages. The writer's siblings were Margaret Alice (Poppie) (1884–1964); (John) Stanislaus (1884–1955), the writer's 'whetstone'; Charles (1886–1941); George Alfred (1887–1902); Eileen (1889–1963); Mary Kathleen (May) (1890–1966); Eva (1891–1957); Florence (1892–1973); Mabel (1893–1911); and Freddie (born and died in 1894). Her son was probably thinking of May Joyce when he called the long-suffering maternal principle of *Finnegans Wake* 'Crippled-with-Children'.

Childhood and schooling

In May 1887 the family moved to 1 Martello Terrace in Bray, co. Wicklow, a rapidly developing seaside resort. The household now included William O'Connell, a widowed uncle of Mr Joyce who had failed in business, and Elizabeth Conway, who was reduced to family dependence when her husband absconded with her inheritance. Called 'Dante' in the family (from 'Auntie'), she served as governess to the children and taught Joyce his letters. There were lively visits from friends including Alf Bergan, Tom Devin, and—a somewhat sensational acquaintance—John Kelly, a Fenian who had been incarcerated by the government and came to recuperate with the Joyces. Kelly was a man of forceful character whose sense of conviction inspired the writer. There were also convivial singing parties with the neighbouring protestant family of James Vance. The young Joyce attended Miss Raynor's infant school with Vance's daughter Eileen.

In 1888 Joyce was sent to Clongowes Wood College, a boarding-school for Catholic gentry at Clane, co. Kildare. He soon acquired the nickname 'Half-Past Six', arising from his answer to a query about his age. As the youngest boy Joyce suffered from homesickness and feelings of insecurity, and the class bully pushed him into a square ditch (a cesspool). He was also beaten on the hands for offences including the use of vulgar language. Father James Daly, the director of studies who administered one such punishment, is the model for Dolan in the *Portrait*, where he is depicted as an ignorant and brutal man. In daring to take his grievance to the rector of the college, Father John Conmee, the young Joyce demonstrated a self-possession and an independence which characterized him throughout his life. The fact that Conmee apologized to him reflected the esteem in which he was already held as a gifted student, although the sincerity of the apology is undermined in the *Portrait*.

The school taught the Jesuits' *ratio studiorum*, the order's counter-Reformational school syllabus, adapted to modern, but not particularly to Irish conditions. The educational ethos was both Catholic and 'west-Briton' in so far as the boys were prepared for the higher ranks of the British imperial administration in Ireland and beyond. Joyce also learned the piano and, though liking cricket, took little part in school games. On 21 April 1889 he made his first holy communion, and he took the name Aloysius at confirmation in spring 1891. Early in October 1891 he appears to have been in the infirmary again, possibly with amoebic dysentery resulting from his immersion in the ditch. This illness may have coincided with the death of Charles Stewart Parnell on 6 October 1891, an event which he conveys through the young boy's fevered vision of his own demise in the *Portrait*. He was taken home, and because of his father's deepening financial problems did not return to Clongowes.

The death of Parnell marked a watershed in Irish cultural and political life, when a new impetus was given to the national movement by W. B. Yeats, Douglas Hyde, and others. The fall of Parnell had been the occasion for a dramatic quarrel in the Joyce household over Christmas dinner when John Stanislaus and Dante clashed over their respective loyalties to the home-rule leader and the Catholic bishops. In the *Portrait* this became one of the most celebrated episodes in modern Irish literature. John Kelly (on whom Mr Casey was modelled) was the catalyst for those violent verbal exchanges, ending with Mr Joyce's grief-stricken cry: 'Poor Parnell! . . . My dead king!' Mrs Conway left the household four days later. It is uncertain whether the dinner row took place in Bray or at Leoville, the new family home at 23 Carysfort Avenue, Blackrock, to which the Joyces were forced to move between late November 1891 and the beginning of 1892, and though the earlier address is favoured in Ellmann's biography, some minor details strongly suggest the latter.

Almost certainly before the removal from Bray however (if not as early as July 1891), Joyce wrote a sentimental elegy for Parnell which his father printed and circulated under the title 'Et tu, Healy'.

By this time John Joyce was in growing trouble at the rates office. Although he courageously defended his collector's pouch from attackers in Phoenix Park in 1887, his mismanagement of funds prompted his transfer to the less congenial North Dock ward area in 1888. In May 1892 the Dublin corporation resolved to take the rates collection office under its own aegis. A series of court actions for settlement of debts culminated in John Joyce's name appearing in *Stubbs' Gazette* on 2 November 1892. This resulted in his immediate suspension from duties by the collector-general, which put his pension settlement in jeopardy, and (tradition has it) it was only after a personal appeal from his wife that a sum of £132 per annum was assigned. In November the Joyces were forced to move to 14 Fitzgibbon Street, Mountjoy Square, a less salubrious address which bordered on the area that Joyce made world-famous as 'Nighttown' in the 'Circe' chapter of *Ulysses*.

Throughout 1892 James Joyce conducted his own
education at home in Blackrock, with some assistance from his mother. Once settled in the city, he
briefly attended the school on North Richmond
Street run by the Christian Brothers—a lowly
order that was social anathema to both father
and son. Release came through the good offices
of Father Conmee, now director of studies at the
Jesuit day school Belvedere College, and on 6 April
1893 James and his brother Stanislaus entered the
school. He faced few intellectual challenges, and
his attitude to his studies was at once compet-
itive and debonair. When he won a £20 award
in intermediate examinations for 1894 he char-
acteristically doled it out in 'loans' to his siblings
and spent even more on a dinner for his parents at a fashionable Dublin restaurant. His poten-
tial as a breadwinner was seized on by the family,
though it was increasingly resisted by the gifted
boy himself, who realized that the 'slight thread
of union' between father and son was breaking
because of the 'gradual rustiness [of] the upper
station' (*Stephen Hero*, 101). The family moved
regularly from 1884 to 1899, in a downward spiral,
and by autumn 1902 were at 7 St Peter's Terrace
in Cabra, the last address Joyce shared with his
father.

Adolescence: shaking the wings

John Joyce's drunkenness and his increasing vio-
lence added to the family's woes: shortly after
the birth and death of Freddie in July 1894
James stopped a physical attack on his mother
by jumping on his father's back. Meanwhile at
school James began to enjoy special favour with
the new rector, Father William Henry, who was
also director of the Sodality of the Blessed Virgin
Mary. On 7 December 1895 Joyce was admitted to
the sodality as a member, and on 25 September
1896 he was elected prefect. His devotion to the
Virgin Mary was evidently sincere, but a shadow
fell across his reputation for devoutness when
Father Henry winkled it out of Stanislaus that
his brother had engaged in spanking games with
a housemaid in his parents' home. Father Henry
warned Mr Joyce that he would have trouble from
the boy, yet that did not prevent his probing
Joyce for signs of a vocation to the priesthood—
an episode which became the turning point in his
relations with the church in the *Portrait*. There
the priest's skull, silhouetted against the window,
together with a noose he makes from the cord of
the 'crossblind', amply prepares the reader for the
young man's realization that 'His destiny was to
be elusive of social or religious orders...to learn

his own wisdom apart from others...wandering among the snares of the world [which] were its ways of sin'.

The annual school retreats at Belvedere, with their sermons on the agonies inflicted on sinful souls by the fiends of hell, instigated in Joyce a period of strict chastity which lasted into spring 1897, when an obsessive round of 'pious ejaculations' (short prayers designed to stave off carnal temptation) on his part, and decades of the rosary by his siblings, were observed. It was not until 1898, when Joyce encountered a 'gay' girl in the street, that he engaged in sexual intercourse in the manner suggested at the close of chapter 2 of the *Portrait*. This sexual experience is juxtaposed with the 'hellfire sermon' that scarifies young Stephen Dedalus.

Joyce's adolescent mood of religious conviction soon gave way to an increasing enthusiasm for modern literature. The works of Thomas Hardy and George Meredith along with the anti-conventional writings of George Bernard Shaw were part of his self-administered diet, but the transforming influence was Henrik Ibsen, whose 'spirit he encounters in a moment of radiant simultaneity', as Joyce later recalled in the autobi-ographical draft novel *Stephen Hero* (1944). Joyce found in Ibsen 'a spirit of wayward boyish beauty' (*Portrait of the Artist as a Young Man*, 179)—a phrase that suggests that his powers of intellectual apprehension were still bounded by the reflexes of *fin de siècle* aestheticism. But much sterner forms of egoism were flexing their muscles—or as Stephen Dedalus would have it, 'shaking the wings of their exultant and terrible youth'. When Joyce saw Hermann Sudermann's *Magda* with his parents in March 1899 he told them that they need not have bothered going to see a play about genius flourishing in the home, since they would soon witness 'genius breaking out' in their own household (Ellmann, *Joyce*, 54).

Such a mind was unlikely to mix easily with other schoolboys, yet aside from defending Byron against asinine criticism in the tussle recounted in chapter 2 of the *Portrait* Joyce was on good terms with his most able peers, including Richard and Eugene Sheehy, sons of the MP David Sheehy. He shared with them musical entertainments, played charades, and mounted burlesque versions of plays and operas. Joyce was generally more reserved than the others, and evinced no partiality

towards girls, though biographers since Ellmann
have asserted that he was shyly infatuated with
Mary, the youngest and reputedly the prettiest
of the Sheehy girls. She is, indeed, the generally
favoured model for Emma Clery in *Stephen Hero*
(Miss M. E. Cleary is another), and her counter-
part, 'E. C.', in the *Portrait*.

Joyce was the educational and social equal of his
contemporaries, but was essentially *déclassé* and
prone to wander deeper into the disreputable side
of Dublin life than any of his friends. Those
odysseys precluded his returning to the ordinary
fold of middle-class youth, and gave him a frankness of appetite, and a desire to find frankness
reciprocated in a way impossible with his educational peers. The obsolescent Parnellite opinions
and improbable gentry pretensions of his father,
both of which Joyce perpetuated in a sublimated
form, provided a further barrier.

Neither Joyce's agnosticism nor his sexual liber-
tinism was known to his mentors at Belvedere,
and he remained to the end a prefect of the
Sodality of the Blessed Virgin Mary. His intellectual interest in mysticism was still sufficient in
October 1897 for him to buy Thomas à Kempis's

Imitation of Christ. Towards the end he fell out with Father Henry when he refused to sit the bishops' examination, considering the senior intermediate a more important occasion. In the event he won £30 for a second year along with £4 for English composition, but failed to win a university exhibition.

manager of a company. He was told that he was a
man who, rather before long, I presumed... cleared all
the changes... anguished... sinosthenic... generator
and... furnishment... more important... weapon to the
... that he won a prize... self-confidence along with
... to... hungered and enured... and failed... to all...
... university students...

'I will let in fresh air'

University years and intellectual development

Having spent a year on the matriculation course of the Royal University of Ireland during 1898–9 Joyce entered University College, Dublin, as an undergraduate in October 1899, reading modern languages with Latin and logic as additional subjects. The reserved but self-possessed young man was acknowledged to be exceptional in both temperament and intellect by his peers. He was certainly the best-read student in his year, yet his examination results were invariably undistinguished and he emerged in 1902 with only a pass degree. He had decided that the college syllabus was far too narrow, and set about educating himself with the help of the National Library of Ireland and Dublin book-barrows.

While at university Joyce took part in the soda-lity's literary conference, attended the Thomas Aquinas Society, and apparently did not leave off Easter duties until his brother George died on 3 May 1902. Up to this point his agnosticism was more a tendency of mind than an intellectual conviction or an artistic premise. He was wary and increasingly disdainful of the Jesuit authorities in the college but responded warmly to individual teachers. The celebrated account of an exchange on the theme of beauty conducted by Stephen with the dean of studies in the *Portrait* reveals a strategy that was by then second nature to him: the use of 'one or two ideas of Aristotle and Aquinas' to frame his own philosophical intuitions. Stephen's colloquy also depicts the young Joyce's growing unease with the condition of received ideas and his heightened awareness of the 'heaps of dead language' (or chichés) around him in the urban world that he inhabited.

The chief of Joyce's friends and associates at University College who modelled for characters in his autobiographical fiction were Vincent Cosgrave, perceptive but coarse of mind (Lynch in the *Portrait*); John Francis (Jeff) Byrne, thoughtful but capable of conventional

disapproval (Cranly in the *Portrait* and *Ulysses*);
George Clancy, a naïve exponent of Irish-Ireland
purismo, later assassinated by the Black and
Tans (Davin in the *Portrait*); Francis Sheehy-
Skeffington, pacificist–feminist–vegetarian and
sporter of knickerbockers, who was murdered in
custody by British soldiers after he quixotically
attempted to prevent looting in the rising of
1916 (McCann in the *Portrait*); and Constantine
Curran, later author on Georgian Dublin archi-
tecture, who produced the most complete memoir
of the period (after Stanislaus Joyce's). The chief
forum for intellectual debate was the Literary and
Historical Society, where Joyce, who was co-opted
to the executive committee, first spoke in January
1899.

Joyce was not, however, training for public and
professional life as the others were: his immediate purpose was to become a recognized writer,
and to that end he composed a review article on
the painting *Ecce homo* by Mihály Munkácsy. On
20 January 1900 Joyce delivered the first of two
papers to the Literary and Historical Society entitled 'Drama and life'. In it he castigated as mis-
taken the insistence on the religious, moral, and
idealizing tendencies of art as well as the 'boyish

instinct to dive under the blankets at the mention of the bogey of realism'. He ended by echoing Lona in Ibsen's play *Samfundets stotter* ('The Pillars of Society'): 'I will let in fresh air'. This clarion call was 'very seriously intended to define his own position for himself', as Joyce wrote in *Stephen Hero*. Its delivery coincided closely with publication of his article 'Ibsen's new drama' in the *Fortnightly Review* (1 April 1900). A fee of 12 guineas enabled him to travel to London with his father and visit William Archer, Ibsen's English translator. He heard from Archer a month later that the playwright had written a note of earnest appreciation when he read the article. Joyce learned Dano-Norwegian so that he could read the plays in the original and write to Ibsen in time for his birthday in March 1901.

Joyce's reading of the works of Gabriele D'Annunzio at this time resulted in a play entitled *A Brilliant Career* dealing with the experience of a young doctor caught up in an epidemic in a midland town. Joyce called it 'the first true work of my life' and dedicated it 'To My Own Soul'. Archer thought it immature. Joyce then turned to the sterner stuff of Gerhart Hauptmann and produced stiff translations of *Vor Sonnenaufgang* and *Michael Kramer* during the following twelve months. (A taste for Hauptmann's drama was later used as an indication of Mr Duffy's emotional sterility in 'A Painful Case'.) Archer was equally discouraging about *Shine and Dark*, Joyce's first poetry collection, which he sent him in September 1901.

About this date Joyce wrote the first of a series of short prose records that he called his epiphanies. He defined the term as 'a sudden spiritual manifestation, whether in the vulgarity of speech or of gesture or in a memorable phase of the mind itself', adding that 'it was for the man of letters to record these epiphanies with extreme care, seeing that they themselves are the most delicate and evanescent of moments' (*Stephen Hero*, 188). The earliest example, preserved with others on the verso of Stanislaus's commonplace book, concerns a butcher-boy observed making a commonplace gesture in Glengariff Parade; others dealt with psychological moments in their author's life and tokens by which his middle-class associates and siblings revealed the ignobility of their minds. What was most important about the technique was, perhaps, the absence of authorial voice: description was cut to a minimum, and hiatus also used for unheard words. The effect was to carry Joyce away from poetry and drama in the generic sense towards a kind of prose which entailed the suggestive power of the one and the actuality of the other. It also posed an epistemological riddle about how the writer gains insight into the 'soul of the object'. The epiphanies that Joyce wrote between 1900 and 1904 were later incorporated into his novels, beginning with the autobiographical draft *Stephen Hero* and ending with *Ulysses*. (The method was revived, though with some alteration in tone, for the manuscript record of a love affair in 1911–14 later published as *Giacomo Joyce*.)

Joyce attended all the productions of the fledgeling Irish Literary Theatre as a student. Yeats's *The Countess Cathleen*, one of the first plays produced in May 1899, was particularly influential. At the deathbed of his brother George in 1902 Joyce sang some lyrics from the play, which he invoked at the end of the 'Nighttown' episode of *Ulysses*. On 14 October 1901 he wrote to protest that Douglas Hyde's *Casadh an tSugáin* and the George Moore–W. B. Yeats collaboration *Diarmuid and Grania* were to be staged in contravention of its professed policy of bringing the best of modern continental drama to the Irish capital. Joyce published the broadside in November 1901, hinting in it that the literary heir to Ibsen who 'Even now ... may be standing by the door' might be himself. In his paper delivered at the Literary and Historical Society on 15 February 1902 on the Irish Romantic poet James Clarence Mangan, Joyce rejected the idea that the rebirth of an Irish nation was a necessary condition of the 'affirmation of the spirit' in literature, and lamented Mangan's plight in writing 'for a public which cared for matters of the day, and for poetry only so far as it might illustrate these'. Whatever else Joyce had to say about nationalist Ireland he reserved for *Stephen Hero*, while he wrote a verse play, 'Dream Stuff' (now lost), and made contact with the leaders of the literary revival. On 18 August 1902 he walked to Rathgar to introduce himself to George Russell (known by the pseudonym Æ), who told him famously that he had not enough chaos in him to be a poet. He met W. B. Yeats in October 1902 and read to him a 'beautiful though immature and eccentric harmony of little prose descriptions and meditations' (Ellmann, *Identity of Yeats*, 86), which Yeats praised. But Joyce professed not to care for Yeats's opinion, and regretted that the poet was too old—a sentiment that he uttered to his face. Joyce also made it abundantly clear that he did not intend to be suborned by the theosophically minded literati gathered around Russell any more than by the nationalist enthusiasts of his own class.

Paris and back

On completion of his studies Joyce followed several college friends into medicine at the Cecilia Street Medical School, Dublin, and on 18 November 1902 applied to the faculty of medicine of the University of Paris. Joyce borrowed money from friends and acquaintances including Lady Gregory, to whom he wrote that he 'found no man yet with a faith like mine' (*Selected Letters*, 8). On her recommendation he was given book reviewing by E. V. Longworth, editor of the Dublin *Daily Express*. His notices on Irish literature over the next six months were uncompromising assertions of his own literary standards. Joyce appraised Lady Gregory's *Poets and Dreamers* as a work in which the author 'has truly set forth the old age of her country ... a land almost fabulous in its sorrow and senility'. Buck Mulligan in *Ulysses* voices the obvious objection:

'She gets you a job on the paper and then you go and slate her drivel to Jaysus. Why can't you do the Yeats touch?'

Joyce reached Paris on 3 December, only to discover that he lacked the necessary qualifications for the faculty of medicine. While in Paris he did however write some epiphanies and amassed the continental experiences which Stephen Dedalus recalls in the 'Nestor' episode of *Ulysses*, notably a cameo of the Jewish traders at the Bourse and a visit to Joseph Casey, formerly a prominent Fenian. Joyce's father found the price of his ticket home in time for Christmas 1902 by raising a further mortgage. In Dublin he met Oliver St John Gogarty, who provided him with an archetypal example of the 'gay betrayer' immortalized as Buck Mulligan in *Ulysses*. Once back in Paris he applied himself to Aristotle's *De anima* in J. Barthélemy Saint-Hilaire's translation (*Psychologie d'Aristote, traité de l'âme*), which he 'Englished' to produce a spare but focused record of philosophical sentences. These anchored his own aesthetic and epistemological syllogisms in the so-called 'Paris notebook' before he resigned them to his autobiographical persona Stephen Dedalus: 'Thought is the thought of thought. Tranquil brightness. The soul is in a manner all that is: the soul is the form of forms.' None the less, bouts of hunger and begging letters home were part of Joyce's life in Paris until the telegram arrived in April 1903 with news that his mother was dying.

Joyce returned to Dublin, but his mother did not die until 13 August; in the interim there were more than the usual distresses, including the out-bursts of his father, who once shouted, 'If you can't get well, die … and be damned to you!' (S. Joyce, *My Brother's Keeper*, 230). Joyce refused to yield to his mother's pleadings that he take the sacraments and later refused even to kneel at her deathbed. May Joyce appears in *Ulysses* as a ghoul terrorizing her son from beyond the grave. In the *Portrait*, where she expresses the hope that he will learn 'what the heart is and what it feels', she is more like her living self and the person-ality expressed in her letters to him in Paris. Her wry scepticism about masculine opinions, and her unfailing pride in and concern for her brilliant but wilful son, produced the only confession of faith he ever made, when he professed to believe in nothing but 'the love of a mother for her child and the love of a man for lies' (Ellmann, *Joyce*, 293). Joyce was greatly affected by his mother's death but remained unsentimental. Following the funeral, at which his father surpassed himself in self-commiseration, Joyce embarked on a series of half-baked plans intended to support a career in literature. He then became a preparatory school teacher for a few weeks in summer 1904 at Clifton School, established in Dalkey by Francis Irwin (Mr Deasy in *Ulysses*).

The experiences of December 1903 to September 1904 make up the immediate background of *Ulysses*. Oliver St John Gogarty helped Joyce to deepen his familiarity with the 'kips' (brothels), and together they refined the arts of bawdy poetry. But Joyce's relationship with Gogarty had become intensely barbed, as each assumed himself superior. Hoping to launch into a singing career, Joyce equipped himself with a respected voice teacher, a first-floor room at Shelbourne Road, and a grand piano. He missed the first prize at the annual Feis Ceoil held in the Antient Concert Rooms on 16 May 1904 because of his inability to sight-sing. On his return to Dublin, Joyce's slight contact with the city's literati had been unamiable: he crashed Lady Gregory's literary gathering and was written off by George Moore, whose poetry he likened to that of Arthur Symons, as a 'beggar'.

The beginnings of *A Portrait of the Artist as a Young Man* and *Dubliners*

But Joyce was far from abandoning writing. On 7 January 1904 he composed in one day an early version of *A Portrait of the Artist as a Young Man*, intended as a contribution to John Eglinton's new journal *Dana*; it was refused as unintelligible. Indeed, the 1904 'Portrait' is meaningless other than as an indicator of Joyce's artistic and imaginative development, and even then it is febrile and obscure. At the outset he speaks of the human personality as 'a fluid succession' of moments, and suggests that this debars literary portraiture of the kind that retails 'beard and inches'. He promises a better way of conveying identity 'through some art, by some process of mind as yet untabulated, to liberate from the personalised lumps of matter that which is their individuating rhythm, the first or formal relation of their parts'. The importance of this declaration is that it links his Aristotelian interests with his search for a literary form that would trace the reality of psychological life, which he here describes as 'the curve of an emotion'.

It was many years before Joyce began to approach that point when, in a bold revision of his

interminable autobiographical novel (the rem-
nant of which appeared posthumously as *Stephen
Hero*), he adopted the method of character-
specific style, moulding the narration to the state
of mind, age, and emotional state of his central
protagonist. In 1904, however, the nascent autobiographical *alter ego* was hardly more than an
explosion of literary and psychic self-importance
which ends by proclaiming:

> Man and woman, out of you comes the nation
> that is to come, the lightning [*sic*] of your
> masses in travail; the competitive order is
> employed against itself, the aristocracies are
> supplanted; and amid the general paralysis of
> an insane society, the confederate will issues in
> action.

There is a sense that James Joyce himself is
expected to be the one 'who would give the word'
to the 'multitudes, not as yet in the wombs of
humanity but surely engenderable there'.

Immediately and over the next few years Joyce
expanded on his essay, and the conviction that 'life
is such as I conceive it.' As *Stephen Hero*, the essay
swelled to 200,000 words before grinding to a halt
in 1913. A panoply of Christological images points

to the messianic stature of the artist. The 'Hero' owed something to Thomas Carlyle's 'Hero as Man of Letters' (a point often contested by Joyce commentators), for he was 'the intense centre of the life of his age to which he stands in a relation than which none can be more vital', as Stephen holds of the true poet and himself. The extant portions (chapters 15–25) roughly correspond to the last chapter of *A Portrait of the Artist as a Young Man*. They deal with Stephen's days at University College, Dublin, and are full of opinions about his teachers and his peers. Anti-clericalism reaches an extraordinary pitch in passages where he compares Ireland's priests to 'black tyrannous lice' who imposed 'Contempt of human nature, weakness, nervous tremblings, fear of day and joy, distrust of man and life, hemiplegia of the will' on those in their power. While his supine contemporaries are reduced to 'terrorized boys, banded together in a complicity of diffidence', he would 'live his own life according to what he recognised as the voice of a new humanity, active, unafraid and unashamed'. Already burdened by this deadening declamation, the novel also suffers from a radical instability of tone. It is impossible to know what the author understands—or expects his reader to understand—by the account that he gives of his literary manner at the date of the events recounted: 'Stephen's style of writing, though it was over affectionate towards the antique and even the obsolete and too easily rhetorical, was remarkable for a certain crude originality of expression.' The trouble is that the style of *Stephen Hero* is entirely of a piece with it.

By way of relief from such an arduous task Joyce assembled a collection of 'Elizabethan' poems, which he called *Chamber Music* (on a scatological hint from Gogarty when they were in earshot of a micturating prostitute). Arthur Symons placed one such poem ('Silently, she's combing') in the *Saturday Review* on 8 April 1904—thus bearing out George Moore's esti-mate of Joyce's poetical character. During the summer of 1904 he began a set of 'epicleti' for the *Irish Homestead*, a newspaper of the Irish co-operative movement fostered by Horace Plun-kett and Æ, which eventually constituted the stories of *Dubliners* (1914). If Æ wanted some-thing 'simple, rural, live-making [with] pathos', what he got was a subtle, damning exposé of the network of hypocrisy and deception, tyranny and abuse, moral cowardice and self-contempt which

Joyce regarded as the symptoms of 'spiritual paralysis' in Ireland. 'The Sisters' (13 August 1904), 'Eveline' (10 September 1904), and 'After the Race' (17 December 1904) appeared successively over the pseudonym Stephen Daedalus, before the editor, H. F. Norman, rumbled the writer's subversive bent and terminated the understanding. 'The Holy Office', written in verse, plotted his relation to the literary revival and the Catholic-nationalist purists of the period; he styled himself 'Katharsis-Purgative' in jejunely Aristotelian terms:

> Thus I relieve their timid arses,
> Perform my office of Katharsis.

Meeting Nora

Joyce's dissolute mode of life had reached an advanced stage when on 10 June 1904, walking in Nassau Street, he was struck by the auburn hair of Nora Barnacle (1884–1951), a chambermaid in Finn's Hotel. Joyce persuaded her to walk out with him in the neighbourhood of the botanical gardens in Ringsend, when on 16 June she offered him the 'kind of satisfaction' that filled him with 'amazed joy' to recollect, as he told her in a letter.

Nora, though still a churchgoing Catholic, was free from the sexual restraints of Joyce's educational class. Joyce supplemented his physical and emotional passion for her with a good deal of intellectual fancy: he came to regard her as his 'soul' and his 'Ireland'—a portable Ireland, as the event would prove. He promptly told her about his religious apostasy and his general disdain for Irish society and his contemporaries, as well as his limitless faith in his own genius. For a while he doubted her response but their unlikely relationship grew closer.

In the summer of 1904 Joyce's living arrangements were unsettled. In September he spent one week in the Martello tower at Sandycove with Gogarty and Samuel Chenevix Trench. This Anglo-Irishman is accurately portrayed as Haines in *Ulysses*, whose dream of panthers provided Gogarty with a pretext to rattle off some shots from his revolver in the main chamber of the tower. Joyce took this as his notice to quit, eventually returning to the family home in Cabra. The Martello tower sojourn forms the basis for the opening of *Ulysses*. As the novel goes on to relate, late in September Joyce met medical friends at the National Maternity Hospital in

Holles Street and proceeded to the 'kips' of the Montgomery Street area in company with Vincent Cosgrave (who earned the name Lynch for standing by when Joyce was beaten in a drunken fight). There Joyce appears to have encountered Alfred Hunter, the model for Leopold Bloom, who rescued him in 'orthodox Samaritan fashion' after he had been beaten by two soldiers. Hunter was an Ulster Presbyterian and commercial traveller who had converted to Catholicism at marriage, but was nevertheless an outsider—though not a Jew as represented in the novel. Joyce later sought detailed information of him from his brother when planning a story to be called 'Ulysses' for the *Dubliners* collection.

By the end of September Joyce was convinced of the hopelessness of staying on in Dublin. Besides lack of money, the strain of his passionate relationship with Nora in an unsympathetic milieu and his increasingly rocky friendships with Constantine Curran and Jeff Byrne precipitated a paranoid sense of isolation which became a recurring note in his dealings with Dublin acquaintances and with publishers. Once he had planned to leave, he accepted Byrne's advice to ask Nora to come with him, rather as Eveline is asked by her untrustworthy lover Frank in the *Dubliners* story named after her. Pausing only to send *Chamber Music* to the publisher Grant Richards the day before they left, the couple reached Paris on 9 October 1904, and then set off for Zürich, where Joyce wrongly understood he had a teaching appointment.

In exile

Trieste and Rome

On reporting to the Berlitz School, Joyce found
no job awaiting him and was sent onwards to
Trieste, in Habsburg Austria. After finding no
post there either, he was redirected to the new
establishment at Pola, under the deputy director
Alessandro Francini. Acclimatization was not easy.
Joyce began by being locked up when he tried to
help three drunken British sailors, and difficulties with money were such that they often moved
before settling at via Giulia 2, near the school.
There Joyce and Nora established the domestic
pattern that characterized their family life for
years to come: intense periods of literary work
alternating with conviviality among colleagues
and pupils, and intermittent bouts of drunkenness.
There was much strain and solitude for Nora, and

a wide gulf of intellectual interests that cut her off from his writing. Joyce had a fascination with her 'untrained' mind, and a delight in her body, which provided him, if not her, with some compensation.

When, early in 1905, Joyce and Nora moved to via Medolino 7, at the invitation of the Francinis, there were eighteen chapters of *Stephen Hero* (Stanislaus received the manuscript for strictly limited circulation among relatives in mid-January 1905). In November Joyce wrote the carefully meditated aesthetic entries of the 'Pola notebook' which turn St Thomas's sentences 'bonum est in quod tendit appetitus' ('the good is that towards the possession of which an appetite tends') and 'pulchra sunt quae visa placent' ('those things are beautiful the apprehension of which pleases') into an ingenious account of the 'act of apprehension', while dismantling the conventional distinction between the 'beautiful' and the 'ugly'. Friendship with Francini flourished to the extent that they embarked on a translation of George Moore's *Celibates* in autumn 1905 while Francini taught Joyce his superior Tuscan in place of the classical Italian that Joyce had learned (so he said) from Dante. But early in March 1905 Joyce's sojourn in Pola, that 'queer old place', was

abruptly terminated when the Austrian authorities expelled all aliens on the discovery of an
Italian spy ring in the city. Having been offered
work at the Berlitz School in Trieste, where he
proved a popular teacher, Joyce settled with Nora
at 31 via San Nicolò, where their son Giorgio
(1905–1976) was born.

As in Pola, Joyce had much time to write, and
he produced nine more stories for the *Dubliners*
collection as well as a spate of letters to Stanislaus
describing his growing affinity with irredentism
and socialism. He was flush enough in June to
have 'The Holy Office' printed for distribution
by his brother in Dublin. The birth of Giorgio
on 27 July 1905 brought domestic strains which
are obliquely reflected in 'A Little Cloud'. But the
'legal fiction' of paternity released in Joyce a new
consciousness of self which led inevitably to the
abandonment of the Dedalian persona and the
adoption of a mentality more like that of Leopold
Bloom. Nora was forced to take in washing, while
Joyce began to drink again, supposedly as a form of
contraception. He embarked on a series of fruitless
money-making schemes, including a new attempt
to make a living as a singer which entailed lessons
with a Triestino teacher and composer, Francesco

Sinico (who remained unpaid and unwittingly bestowed his name on the tragic central figure of 'A Painful Case' in *Dubliners*). In October Stanislaus joined the household, and acted as his 'brother's keeper' at endless sacrifice to himself until the First World War. The arrangement brought its own tensions, and Stanislaus turned into a resentful memorialist. In February 1906 the Joyce ménage moved to via Giovanni Boccaccio, sharing with the Francinis, by then also established in Trieste.

On 3 December 1905 Joyce sent twelve stories to Grant Richards, who agreed to publish them as a collection, thus setting in motion an eight-year saga which Joyce later described as the 'fiasco' of *Dubliners*. Encouraged at this time, he quickly added two more stories, 'Two Gallants' and 'A Little Cloud', while carefully revising 'A Painful Case' and 'After the Race'. On 23 April 1906 Richards wrote to say that his printer had red-pencilled the epithet 'bloody' in 'Two Gallants', and in ensuing exchanges further objectionable passages were noted, including aspersions on the prince of Wales and—more likely to offend the censor—sado-masochistic hints in 'An Encounter'. Richards revoked the agreement in September

1906. In letters to the publisher that summer, Joyce defended his stories as a 'first step towards the spiritual liberation of [his] country' (*Letters*, 1.63), in the portrayal of the 'centre of paralysis' that was Dublin. In the same spirit he disclaimed responsibility for the 'odour of ashpits and old weeds and offal' (ibid., 1.64) which hung about his stories on the grounds that no artist dares 'alter in the presentment what he has seen or heard' while condemning the censorship laws of England.

In August 1906 Joyce took up a post in the international banking house of Nast-Kolb and Schumacher in Rome. Nora's and Joyce's seven-month stay in Rome taxed Joyce's resources, nerves, and relationship with Nora (which he considered to be a marriage) more than any other period of his self-styled 'exile' so far. Hours at the bank were long and the work entirely unsympathetic. He found a private pupil before taking on part-time hours at the École des Langues late in November 1906. He frequently dined out and drank without coming to like the city any better, comparing its denizens to a man who makes his living by exhibiting his grandmother's corpse. No progress was made with *Stephen Hero*, and his interest in *Dubliners* began to wane. 'A Painful Case' and 'After the Race', in particular, now seemed poor stuff to him. In Trieste he had contemplated a collection called *Provincials* to follow *Dubliners*; yet in Rome he conceived several new stories in the urban vein, 'The Last Supper', 'The Street', 'Vengeance', 'At Bay', and 'Catharsis', and planned one other called 'Ulysses'. This 'never got forrarder than its title' as a short story, but came to serve as the germ for the novel of that name. By Christmas, however, Joyce was working on 'The Dead', a final story for the stalled collection *Dubliners*. This classic example of the genre was inspired by a growing sense that he had underrated the tradition of hospitality in his native city, and supplied a redemptive air at the end without diminishing the emphasis on 'paralysis' that governs all the stories.

On 7 January 1907 the publisher Elkin Mathews wrote to propose terms for the publication of *Chamber Music*. Joyce took this as an omen and abruptly resigned from the bank with effect from 5 March. But Rome had not finished with Joyce yet: *Dubliners* was rejected by John Long on 21 February, and shortly before his departure Joyce was mugged in the street, losing 200 crowns. He returned to Trieste and the Berlitz School in early March, his mouth 'full of decayed teeth' and his soul full of 'decayed ambitions'. In addition, Nora was pregnant again notwithstanding their habit of sharing the bed head-to-toe—the method of contraception also practised by Leopold and Molly in *Ulysses*.

Lectures and publication

The Joyces settled at via S. Caterina, sharing cramped quarters there until a row over debts resulted in Stanislaus's moving out in autumn 1908. Joyce taught reluctantly for a lowly rate. He was commissioned by his pupil Roberto Prezioso to write three articles on Ireland in Italian for *Il Piccolo della Sera*: 'Il Fenianismo: l'ultimo feniano' (22 March), 'Home rule maggiorenne' (19 May), and 'L'Irlanda all sbarra' (16 September 1907). At the invitation of Dr Attilio Tamaro, another pupil, Joyce presented three lectures at the Università Popolare in April–May 1907: 'Irlanda, isola dei santi et dei savi', 'Giacomo Clarenzio Mangan' (May 1907), and a third on the Irish literary revival (now lost). In addressing a Triestino public with strongly irredentist leanings, Joyce showed himself surprisingly unwilling to advance the claims of Irish nationhood against those of British unionism. Ireland was not a new country asserting its independence, but 'a very old country' trying 'to renew under new forms the glories of a past civilisation'. In this archaic guise he doubted whether the Irish nationalists could establish a modern state of the sort he might wish to inhabit. In addition, he bore the old Parnellite grudge against parliamentary nationalists and equally, while clearly admiring its determination, he discounted the military capacity of Fenianism, the 'physical force' movement which he expressly identified with Sinn Féin. Ascribing blame to the colonial regime interested him less than understanding the paralysed condition of his country— hence his assertion that, while Ireland's 'soul has been weakened by centuries of useless struggles and broken treaties', the real deficit lay in the fact that the 'economic and intellectual conditions do not permit the development of individuality'. Separatist politics were marred by a 'hysterical nationalism', and cultural revivalism by an equally fantastical delusion, since in his view 'Ancient Ireland is dead just as ancient Egypt is dead'.

Joyce considered Anglo-Saxon and Roman Catholic authority to be equally 'foreign powers' in Ireland. In his lecture on Mangan—a version of the one he gave in Dublin five years earlier—he warned that 'The poet who would hurl his lightning against tyrants would establish upon the future a crueller and more intimate tyranny', thus revealing his suspicions of the form of stateship that an independent Ireland might embody. There is an obvious reference to himself in the melodramatic assertion that 'No one who has any self-respect stays in Ireland, but flees afar as though from a country that has undergone the visitation of an angered Jove'. Yet the difference between 'flight' and the notion of the artist in exile that he cultivated in Trieste is less significant than that between Joyce's insistence that Ireland remain the hamstrung nation which he left and the attempts, constitutional or otherwise, of those at home to remedy the situation. The well-known pacificism of certain episodes in *Ulysses* has its origins in such differences—as has the vagary that Bloom keeps a furled union flag near the ingleside of his front room. In his journalism of 1907 Joyce showed himself out of step with his Irish contemporaries, and preferred to remain so even at the cost of being out of step with his Triestino neighbours.

With *Chamber Music* Joyce became a published writer in May 1907, but not before he had considered withdrawing the thirty-six poems in view of their archaic air and literary slightness. The book was generously reviewed by Arthur Symons but was largely ignored by readers, fewer than 200 copies selling in the ensuing five years, though Geoffrey Molyneux Palmer requested permission to set the lyrics to music. As Nora's term approached, Joyce drank more than previously and was rescued from the gutter on one occasion by Francini. Financial hardship was such that he even applied for a post with the South Africa Colonisation Society early in July, but he was soon ill with rheumatic fever. On 26 July 1907, while he lay in one bed in the Ospedale Civico, Nora gave birth to their daughter (Anna) Lucia in the paupers' maternity ward. The child had a perceptible squint, about which she became very self-conscious as she grew older.

Joyce's illness actually spurred creative activity, and he emerged from hospital with the text of 'The Dead', which he completed on 6 September 1907. During convalescence he planned future writing including—at least in embryo—*Ulysses* (he told Stanislaus that the novel would be a Dublin *Peer Gynt*). He also planned to rewrite *Stephen Hero* in five long chapters, leaving out the sections leading up to schooldays. By 29 November he had finished the first chapter of what became *A Portrait of the Artist as a Young Man*. When Artifoni leased the Berlitz School, Joyce took on his own private pupils, among them Ettore Schmitz, who wrote as Italo Svevo and received crucial encouragement from his friend Joyce.

Dubliners: a curious history

In April 1909 Joyce sent the manuscript of *Dubliners* to George Roberts at Maunsel, in Dublin, and in July he returned there. He looked in vain to his friend Tom Kettle to secure him a post at University College, and a meeting with Vincent Cosgrave proved painfully shocking. His claim to have enjoyed Nora's favours while Joyce was courting her in Dublin triggered an acute attack of jealousy in Joyce, who bombarded Nora with letters questioning her virginity, his paternity, and the trust upon which their relationship was founded, asking her on 6 August, 'is it all over between us?' Byrne assured him that the whole episode was the result of a plot between Cosgrave and Gogarty to break his spirit. Joyce's next letters to Nora were full of self-abasement and erotic longing. The event had however sparked off a train of thought on the question of jealousy, the subject of his play *Exiles*. After an initial meeting with George Roberts he signed a contract for *Dubliners* with Joseph Maunsel Hone, and managed to extract an advance of £300 from Roberts. On 13 September he returned to Trieste with his sister Eva (who went back to Dublin in July 1911).

Joyce's mind turned again to money-making schemes, and he went into partnership with Triestino businessmen to establish a cinema in Dublin. After returning there in October, he found suitable premises at 45 Mary Street and fitted them with electricity, gained a licence, and recruited staff. When two of the partners came over to complete the business they lodged initially in Finn's Hotel. A visit to Nora's former room stimulated Joyce to write her a letter in a lyrical tone that characterizes the final chapter of the *Portrait*. As the separation from her lengthened, his letters expressing sado-masochistic impulses compounded by coprophiliac tendencies and an obsession with women's underwear summoned a willing response in Nora. The Volta Cinema opened on 20 December 1909, first showing films such as *The Tragic Story of Beatrice Cenci*, which were received with general enthusiasm but had limited appeal for an Anglophone audience. The Volta later succumbed to the influx of more exciting fare from America, and in July 1910 it was peremptorily sold off at 40 per cent loss to the investors. Before departing Joyce secured an agency from the Dublin Woollen Company to import tweed to Trieste.

Back in Trieste by January 1910 with his sister Eileen, Joyce resumed teaching, though he passed the mornings 'at his thoughts' in bed. His relations with George Roberts deteriorated after the publisher insisted on changes to *Dubliners*. Joyce eventually agreed, but when Roberts pronounced them inadequate Joyce wrote on 10 July threatening to take legal action against the publisher. A letter from Roberts in December bore a promise of publication on 20 January 1911 and gave notice that proofs for *Dubliners* were on the way, but they were never sent. Roberts wrote again in February 1911 renewing his objections to 'Ivy Day in the Committee Room' and calling for more radical revision. Joyce's frustration reached such a pitch that he allegedly threw the manuscript of the *Portrait* in the fire, from where it was rescued by Eileen. (The story was relayed by Samuel Beckett to the later editor of the manuscript but the surviving pages show no scorch marks.) At the beginning of August, Joyce wrote to King George V to find out whether he objected to the contested phrases about Edward VII in 'Ivy Day' and received a predictably anodyne letter from his secretary. He then sent Roberts an open letter documenting the history of *Dubliners* which was printed in the *Northern Whig* (Belfast) in late August and in *Sinn Féin* (Dublin) in early September 1911.

In March 1912 Joyce gave a second series of lectures at the Università Popolare entitled 'Verismo ed idealismo nella letteratura inglese: Daniele De Foe e William Blake'. His account of each author maps out the territories in which he was coming to stake his own claim as a writer as well as prefiguring the mind and temperament of Leopold Bloom and Stephen Dedalus in complex and interchangeable ways. In April he took examinations to become a teacher in the state school system, but his admission to the profession was blocked by the unwillingness of the authorities to acknowledge his British university degree.

In July Joyce joined Nora in Dublin to try to settle the matter of *Dubliners*. Together at Oughterard in co. Galway they visited the grave of Michael Bodkin, the young boy who had 'died for her' as related in 'The Dead'. Joyce, who was moved to see a grave inscribed for one 'J. Joyce' nearby, wrote the moving poem 'She Weeps for Rahoon'. Their two days on the Aran Islands resulted in an article for *Il Piccolo della Sera* in which Joyce evinced a new interest in native Irish life and folklore. Face to face with George Roberts again, Joyce found that his arguments in favour of the collection as it stood resulted in a demand for a bond of £1000 to indemnify the publisher against libel. Joyce's friend Tom Kettle declared the stories harmful to Ireland and promised to 'slate' them if they appeared. He particularly disparaged 'An Encounter', and Joyce agreed to delete it. On 18 August he suffered a further set-back when Padraic Colum called 'An Encounter' a 'terrible story'. Fortified by this, the Maunsel publisher demanded the wholesale omission of several other stories.

Joyce engaged a solicitor who wrote a damning legal opinion warning that the vigilance committee would set upon the collection. Roberts's own solicitor warned of libel charges and advised two sureties of £500. At this point Joyce pawned his watch and chain to stay in Dublin. On 30 August Roberts—by now toying with him—responded to Joyce's point-by-point defence by demanding that he rewrite whole paragraphs in 'Grace', 'Ivy Day', and 'The Boarding House' as well as changing every proper name in the book. When, on 5 September, Roberts finally offered to sell the galleys of *Dubliners* for £30, Joyce accepted on a ten-day bill to be paid from Trieste, planning to publish the collection under his own imprint, which he would call the Liffey Press. At this point Joyce apparently secured one set 'by a ruse', as he later wrote. In the event, the printer, John Falconer, refused to part with the galleys when asked on 10 September, and the following day he destroyed 1000 sets of the so-called 1910 Maunsel edition of *Dubliners*. Joyce left Dublin with his family on the same evening, and stopped briefly in London to offer the book to the *English Review* and Mills and Boon. He never returned to Ireland.

At Flushing station in the Netherlands, Joyce wrote 'Gas from a Burner', a verse invective replete with allusions to fatuous and supine practices of Dublin publishers and literati, printed in Trieste shortly after his return. In the meantime Stanislaus had rented a new apartment at

4 via Donato Bramante, after the Joyces had been evicted from their previous residence; it became their home for the remainder of their time in Trieste. Joyce took up a post at the Scuola Revoltella Superiori de Commercio in 1913, but continued afternoon lessons at the homes of private pupils. One of these was Amalia Popper, possibly the object of those yearnings which formed the basis of a new collection of epiphanies written between 1911 and 1914 and ultimately published in 1968 as *Giacomo Joyce*—after the ironic name he used for the slightly aged lover faced with the bittersweet discovery that 'youth has an end'. Lessons with Paolo Cuzzi's younger sister and her teenage friends ended abruptly when Signora Cuzzi caught Joyce and the girls sliding down the bannisters after the lesson.

Joyce lectured on *Hamlet* at the Università Popolare between 11 November 1912 and 11 February 1913. Throughout 1913 his preparatory work on *Exiles* and *Ulysses* continued alongside *Giacomo Joyce* (several epiphanies from which were used in the novel when he had resolved against issuing it as a discrete literary text). Martin Secker and Elkin Mathews having refused *Dubliners*, Joyce wrote to Grant Richards, who wrote back. In

December 1913 his fortunes changed. Both W. B. Yeats and Ezra Pound were struck by Joyce's poem 'I Hear an Army', which Pound wanted to reprint in his anthology *Des Imagistes*. Joyce sent a revised first chapter of the *Portrait* to him, along with the manuscript of *Dubliners*. Pound was so impressed that he immediately placed the novel with *The Egoist*, an originally feminist journal edited by Dora Marsden and Harriet Shaw Weaver. Joyce's explanation of the publishing history of *Dubliners*, which included his letter to the Irish press, appeared as 'A Curious History' in the January issue of *The Egoist*. The first chapter of the *Portrait* began to appear in the next, coming out on Joyce's birthday and thus establishing a tradition to which he adhered for the rest of his career. It also established the pattern that characterized the publication of *Ulysses* and *Finnegans Wake*. Publishing serially in journals gave Joyce the opportunity to revise his work endlessly, and to evolve the idea of the modern novel as a 'work in progress' which in its most extreme form was never fully 'finalized'.

Emboldened by his success with the *Portrait*, Joyce asked Richards for an immediate decision, and received his undertaking on 29 January 1914 to publish *Dubliners*. The agreement signed in March committed Joyce to taking the first 120 copies and gave Richards first option on his next work. Richards used page proofs from the Maunsel edition as copy for the first edition, which was published in 1250 copies on 15 June. Meanwhile serialization of the *Portrait* in *The Egoist* continued between February and August 1914; in the August issue one passage which offended the printer ('Fresh Nelly is waiting on you') was removed. Serialization was completed under a different printer between November 1914 and 1 September 1915.

Portrait and *Ulysses*

The war years

On 1 March 1914 Joyce began the long-prepared
writing of *Ulysses*, without abandoning the composition of *Exiles*, which had developed its own
momentum by this time. (He also worked part-
time as English correspondent to the Gioacchino
Veneziani paint factory.) Joyce's *annus mirabilis*,
however, coincided with the outbreak of European
war. In January 1915 Stanislaus was arrested as
an outspoken irredentist, and in August he was
interned for the duration of the war. Notwithstanding their British citizenship, Joyce and Nora
remained unaffected until Italy declared war on
Germany in May 1915. The Austrian authorities began a partial evacuation of Trieste. Eileen,
now married, moved to Prague. Joyce managed to
gain American visas from the US consulate then

57

catering for British citizens in the region, and the Joyces were permitted to leave Austria for Switzerland, where they reached Zürich on 30 June 1915. With him Joyce had the manuscript of 'Calypso', possibly the first episode of *Ulysses* to be written.

On entering Switzerland Joyce, with no Stanislaus to depend on, was virtually without money. Through the solicitude of Pound and Yeats he received £75 from the Royal Literary Fund, and through Siegmund Feilbogen, editor–proprietor of the *International Review*, he took on editorial work for some months at the end of 1915. Although he spent recklessly, his income increased during the war years as a result of the indulgence of his pupils (who often paid for lessons that they did not receive) and the munificence of patrons. The sum of £100 reached Joyce from the civil pension list in August 1916, while Pound secured a further £2 weekly from the Society of Authors. Late in February 1917 he received notification from an English solicitor that he was to receive a quarterly income of £50 from an anonymous admirer, who turned out to be Harriet Shaw Weaver of *The Egoist*. Miss Weaver also settled on him £5000 in war loan bonds in May 1919. From March 1918 to October 1919 he received a monthly stipend of 1000 francs from Mrs Edith Rockefeller McCormick, but the payments ended after he refused her request that he be psychoanalysed by Carl Jung. (Joyce was always sceptical about psychoanalysis, and caricatured its chief exponents as the 'Swiss Tweedledum' and the 'Viennese Tweedledee'; *Selected Letters*, 282.) All of this Joyce accepted as his due, spending his time at operas and concerts, and with Frank Budgen—a painter working for the Ministry of Information whom he met in 1918, and who subsequently wrote *James Joyce and the Making of 'Ulysses'* (1934) guided by Joyce himself. At the height of these regalements the Joyce children complained that they were left at home unattended.

There were madcap schemes in Zürich also. In spring 1917 Joyce was caught up in a plan of Jules Martin (real name Juda de Vries) to form a film company in order to extract funds from wealthy women intent on appearing in their films. (Before the year was out Martin had been arrested for embezzlement.) Irregular living—Joyce was drinking absinthe at the time—led to increasingly frequent attacks of the iritis which he had experienced first in Trieste and later in Dublin during summer 1912. In mid-August he was diagnosed with glaucoma and synechia. During convalescence from an iridectomy on his right eye Joyce suffered a nervous collapse and recovered in Locarno from October 1917 to January 1918. Yet throughout this period writing of *Ulysses* went on relentlessly. Friends were constantly drawn in as conversational sounding boards, couriers, and typists. One such was Claud Sykes, an actor whom Joyce had met through the abortive film company scheme. During November and December 1917 Joyce sent back to Zürich the first three chapters of *Ulysses*, and Sykes produced the typescript, which was forwarded to Pound for serial publication.

Joyce's reputation as a writer of stature was advancing steadily all the while among the 'little magazines' through the dogged literary networking of his supporters. In May 1914 Grant Richards, however, decided not to exercise his option on the *Portrait* for lack of an audience in time of war, and it was rejected by Secker in July 1915. Through J. B. Pinker, his literary agent from February 1915, Joyce secured Richards's sales of *Dubliners*: disappointingly, by mid-1915 only 525 copies had been sold. In January 1916 Edward Garnett radically misjudged the originality of the

Portrait, regarding it as a formless piece of work, and rejected it for Duckworth. Reeling from this, Joyce instructed Pinker to place the *Portrait* with Miss Weaver following an offer made the previous November, although no printer could be found after D. H. Lawrence's *The Rainbow* (1915) was banned for obscenity. At this juncture B. W. Huebsch agreed to publish it in New York if Miss Weaver would take 750 copies from him for publication in England. With this agreement in place by October, *A Portrait of the Artist as a Young Man* appeared on 29 December 1916 in New York and on 22 January 1917 in London.

Ulysses: epic, cycle, and little story

In the *Portrait* Joyce had brought to its furthest development the 'embryological' method of tracing the development of his hero's 'soul' that he had glimpsed in the 1904 'Portrait' essay. The 'young man' embraces by turns religious ardour and literary aestheticism and finally discovers in himself the capacity and the will to 'forge in the smithy of [his] soul the uncreated conscience of [his] race'. This sentence, which provides an intellectual climax to the novel, is very like another that Joyce actually wrote to Nora during his struggles with George Roberts in 1912 when he spoke of 'creating a conscience' of this 'wretched race' despite the perfidy that surrounded him. To draw out the line of his own artistic development further, however, Joyce had to wrench himself free from the unlimited egoism of Stephen Dedalus, who, as he told Frank Budgen, during the writing of *Ulysses* had 'a shape that can't be changed' (Budgen, 105). It is difficult to know exactly when Joyce arrived at this new estimate of the character whose creation and development had engaged him for ten years before he wrote '1904–1914' at the bottom of the last page of the *Portrait*. Certainly there are signs that he regarded the messianic self-exaltation of his *alter ego* as a dangerous show of hubris, comically foreshadowing the 'lapwing poet' that Stephen became in the opening chapters of *Ulysses*, where he is more like Icarus than like the masterful 'old artificer' Daedalus.

Yet, along with the shift in values that brought Leopold Bloom into existence as a counterbalance to the youthful hero in *Ulysses*, the abandonment of a privileged standpoint from which the social world could be surveyed and judged plunged Joyce into an epistemological maelstrom.

He was, of course, never seriously tempted to adopt the narratorial voice of an urbane, knowing author. The colonial experience from which he sprang dictated that the only authentic representation of reality in language must follow the contours of a divided world (not that colonialism *per se* would be his subject). In *Ulysses* he played remorsely out the logic of the historical legacy of cultural and psychological division which is the true legacy of the colonial epoch (and a chief resource of leading Irish writers). In Joyce's case, formal and stylistic experimentalism is the signature of that legacy. None of his original supporters in the Anglo-American world of letters—Pound, Eliot, and Miss Weaver—could accept that experimentalism should be taken so far, and there was a parting of the ways after the 'Sirens' chapter in which his *fuga per canonem* struck Pound as wilful and absurd. But Joyce believed in his perception that what we know as reality, like religious doctrine, is founded 'on the incertitude of the void'—the void being the phenomenal diversity of human perceptions, points of view, *Weltanschauungen*, habits of expression, intentionalities, and idiolects. This intense relativism is unsustainable without a corresponding belief that the relativized order of experience overlies a spiritual unity accessible only through the multiplex channels of living language.

Just as the radically socialized world of *Ulysses* developed from the *Portrait*, so *Ulysses* led on to the cosmic universe of *Finnegans Wake*, in which all diversity is bound into a vast system of correspondences: mythic, stereotypical, accidental, homophonic, but always testimony to the 'continual affirmation of the human spirit' (a phrase which Joyce used in his essay on Mangan and in *Ulysses* and *Stephen Hero*). The plot and execution of *Ulysses* make it clear that the human spirit can be affirmed by two means, thought and action; and by two types, the artist and the 'citizen'. When, in the penultimate chapter, Joyce represents Stephen and Bloom at the moment before parting, pouring out their 'sequent, then simultaneous urinations' by the faint glow of a bedroom window, he is able to square the circle by demonstrating that what seems divided is actually united and what seems united is perpetually falling into division. Significantly, the two are standing in the garden, dimly lit by 'The heaventree of stars hung with humid nightblue fruit'—an arrangement that recalls the end of Dante's *Purgatorio*. At the same time the faintly illumined presence of Molly in the position of a moon is a symbol of the eternal female whose sensual affirmation in the last word of the novel ('yes') stands for the continual *exitus et reditus*, the coming and going, of human love, 'that word known to all men'.

Serialization in the *Little Review* undoubtedly contributed to the growing complexity of style that made *Ulysses* the ultimate work of literary experimentalism prior to *Finnegans Wake*. In each episode Joyce carried formal invention further than before, and was increasingly obliged to explain to his patrons and supporters the reasons for those methods which were so much at variance with Pound's promotion of him as the 'nearest thing we have to Flaubertian prose in English' (*The Egoist*, 4/2, February 1917, 21–2). In September 1920 he defended his novel to Miss Weaver: '[*Ulysses*] is my epic of two races and at the same time the cycle of the human body as well as a little story of a day', adding:

It is also a sort of encyclopaedia. My intention is to transpose the myth *sub specie temporis nostri*. Each adventure (that is, every hour, every organ, every art being interconnected and interrelated in the structural scheme of the whole) should not only condition but even create its own technique. (*Letters*, 1.146–7)

In June 1921 he still struggled to justify the daunting texture of the novel:

> The task I set myself technically in writing a book from eighteen different points of view and in as many styles, all apparently unknown or undiscovered by my fellow tradesmen, that and the nature of the legend chosen[,] would be enough to upset anyone's mental balance. (*Selected Letters*, 284)

Joyce nevertheless insisted to Frank Budgen that though the methods were complicated, the thought was always simple.

Apart from Joyce's governing theme—the necessary place of love in human society—an important factor was his steady adherence to the Homeric parallel, taking the simplified narrative in Charles Lamb's *The Adventures of Ulysses*, which he read as a child, as a template for a very modern novel. Behind this lay a conviction that Odysseus, not Christ (or any other hero), was the proper model for modern man: sceptical yet able, longing for home when away and aching to wander when at home; uxorious but open to erotic stimulus and female blandishment. Such a conception involved an imaginative and occasionally jejune review of the *Odyssey* and all related texts, in antiquity and later times, notably those of Victor Bérard and other pioneers of modern archaeology and classical exegesis.

At times Joyce's hermeneutic method was unashamedly whimsical—he turns the brand with which Odysseus blinds the Cyclops into a 'knockmedown cigar'. But that simply demonstrates that he kept his gaze fixed on the image of a modern man who, though unaided by any dogma other than his belief in his moral superiority, can face life's challenges with adequate understanding and practical assurance. Exploring this idea in the 'Ithaca' chapter, Joyce proffered his most ingenious, perspicacious, and light-hearted contrivance when Leopold Bloom finds he has left his latchkey in his other trousers and must let himself in by dropping into the front area of his house. Just when Stephen is affirming his own nature as 'an animal proceeding syllogistically from the known to the unknown and a conscious rational reagent between a micro- and a macrocosm ineluctably constructed upon the incertitude of the void', Bloom finds himself 'comforted' by the apprehension 'that as a competent keyless citizen he had proceeded energetically from the unknown to the known through the incertitude of the void'.

Ulysses first appeared in the *Little Review* (USA), edited by Margaret Anderson and Jane Heap, between March 1918 and December 1920. In the opening chapters ('Telemachus', 'Nestor', and 'Proteus'), Stephen Dedalus begins his hegira from the Martello tower to the school in Dalkey where he teaches for the last time, and goes onwards to the city, 'walking into eternity along Sandymount Strand'. 'Calypso' and 'Lotus-Eaters', appearing in June and July 1918, introduced the reader to Leopold and Marion (Molly) Bloom, starting the day at their house in Eccles Street. Bloom crosses the city to the Westland Row post office to collect a letter from his clandestine correspondent Martha, before entering the turkish baths. The 'Hades' episode, set at Glasnevin cemetery, was published in September 1918, with 'Aeolus' appearing the month later. 'Lestrygonians' (January–March 1919), which takes the characters as far as lunchtime in the single day that spans the whole of the novel, was the first

to raise real misgivings about the 'arsthitic' tendency of *Ulysses*, as Pound called it, suggesting
in his pun that Joyce's artistic integrity was being
compromised by his attention to lower matters.
Katherine Mansfield and Virginia Woolf thought
the author 'low-bred' for all his self-evident
genius.

'Scylla and Charybdis' (April–May 1919), which
takes Stephen Dedalus to the National Library
of Ireland, was followed by 'Wandering Rocks'
(June–July 1919), a *tour de force* in literary logis-
tics. The movements of the characters are carefully timed by Joyce, who asked friends in Dublin
how long the different itineraries would take. In
'Sirens' (August–September 1919), stylistic experimentalism begins in earnest. The device of *fuga
per canonem* rests on a questionable analogy
between the musical and literary arts. It was, however, the phallocentric eroticism of the chapter
that alienated its contemporary readers. 'Cyclops'
(November 1919–March 1920) is a brilliant parody
of Irish nationalism in the personage of Michael
Cusack, founder of the Gaelic Athletic Association
(here called 'the citizen'), and the Irish-Ireland
mania of which he is a prime representative.

'Nausicaa' (April–August 1920) was started in Zürich and continued in Trieste in October 1919. Following a period of three weeks during which he claimed not to have read, written, or spoken, Joyce resumed working on the chapter in November and finished it in time for his thirty-eighth birthday in February 1920. The episode centres on Gerty MacDowell, a lame girl who leads Leopold Bloom on through the 'wondrous revealment' of her 'nansook knickers'. (Early in 1919 Joyce was sexually drawn to Marthe Fleischmann, an attractive young woman with a slight limp who reminded him of a girl he had seen in Clontarf in 1898.) In 'Nausicaa' Joyce evolved the technique that he characterized in a letter to Frank Budgen as 'namby-pamby jammy marmalady drawersy (*alto là*!)', examples of which could be found in novelettes and hymnbooks he asked his Aunt Josephine to send from Dublin. (Hearing that his aunt thought *Ulysses* unfit to read, he said: 'If *Ulysses* isn't fit to read, life isn't fit to live'; Ellmann, *Joyce*, 537.) 'Oxen of the Sun' (September–December 1920), which proved to be the last serialized portion of the novel, has Stephen and Bloom in the National Maternity Hospital on very different pretexts. In it Joyce parodied canonical prose styles to highlight the embryological development of English. The result is a literary fabric which he frankly admitted to be the 'most difficult ... to interpret and to execute' in his odyssey of style so far (*Letters*, 1.137). It is also the most resolutely Aristotelian. T. S. Eliot considered it a revelation of the 'futility of all styles'—a judgement related to his own conviction that the 'mythic method' of *Ulysses* was 'a way of controlling, of ordering, of giving shape and a significance to the immense panorama of futility and anarchy which is contemporary history' (Eliot, 201). It is far from certain that Joyce shared Eliot's anxiety.

The composition of 'Circe'—a *Walpurgisnacht* in which Stephen and Bloom confront their inner demons in the brothel quarter of Dublin— engaged Joyce from June to December 1920, spanning the period of his move to Paris in October 1920. Like the remaining three chapters, it did not appear in print until the publication of the completed novel in February 1922. 'Eumaeus' follows Stephen and Bloom from Nighttown to the cabman's shelter, where questions of history and politics visit their tired minds. It is a skilful sampler of clichés and misleading information from the social and political consciousness of contemporary Ireland together with a peculiarly Joycean vision of Parnell and the Invincibles. 'Ithaca' is conducted in catechetical form—an encyclopaedia crossed with family charades and tinged with cosmological awe. It brings Stephen and Bloom to Bloom's kitchen, before the younger man goes out into the night to become (presumably) the author of *Ulysses* ten years later. In 'Penelope' Joyce created a virtually unpunctuated stream of consciousness: the unexpurgated contents of Molly Bloom's mind flow around the day's events and the events of other days, finally returning to Leopold, whom she recalls choosing because he 'understood or felt what a woman is and I knew I could always get round him'. Her life-affirming 'yes' added in October 1921 is conditional, but an affirmation none the less. (Inspiration came from Lillian Wallace, the wife of his friend Richard Wallace, who repeatedly employed the 'yes' in conversation.) After long meditation, Joyce had written *Ulysses*, mostly in Zürich. This gave Tom Stoppard grounds for the retort he puts in the novelist's mouth in *Travesties* (1974), where he rebuts a rhetorical question as to what he did during the war with the smart answer, 'I wrote *Ulysses*. What did you do?'

Publication of *Ulysses*

During the Zürich years Joyce had formed a theatrical company, the English Players, with Claud Sykes. The first production was Wilde's *The Importance of Being Earnest* at the Theater zu den Kaufleuten on 29 April 1918. The evening was a success largely owing to the acting of Henry Carr, who had a minor post in the consulate, but Carr was upset to receive so small a share of the profits, and pursued Joyce in the courts. Joyce won the first case on 15 October 1918 but lost the second on 11 February 1919, with costs and damages totalling 120 francs. Fortunately there soon arrived gifts of $1000 from millionaire friends of Padraic and Mary Colum in New York, from which Joyce paid $200 towards the upkeep of the English Players. In spring 1919 his attempts to stage Purcell's *Dido and Aeneas* were hindered by the British consulate, which confirmed his contempt for such officials. In *Ulysses* Carr's name was used for the coarse and belligerent soldier in the 'Circe' episode and that of Horace Rumbold, British minister to Switzerland, for the semi-literate hangman. Notwithstanding Carr's defection, Joyce took the English Players on tour to Lausanne, Geneva, Montreux, and Interlaken. In mid-June the company staged Synge's *Riders to the Sea*, with Nora as Catheleen. His own play *Exiles* reached the stage in a German translation by Hannah von Mettal, made at the instigation of Stefan Zweig. Produced as *Verbannte* in Munich on 7 August 1919, it ran for only one night, adjudged 'a flop' by Joyce to forestall criticism.

On 19 October Joyce returned to Trieste with his family and moved in with his sister Eileen at 2 via Sanità, where Stanislaus was already ensconced, having been released from internment. Joyce gave a few lessons at the Istituto di Commercio 'Revoltella' (the last time he taught), and socialized with Ettore Schmitz and the Francinis—though Clotilde Francini found his manner altered. Relations with Stanislaus were cooler too; indeed, the brothers were never close again. Stanislaus's resentment of Joyce's exploitation over many years and his disappointment with Joyce's recent works were beginning to harden in Stanislaus's mind. Joyce's view is portrayed in the Shem–Shaun relationship of *Finnegans Wake*, in which the over-regulated and authoritarian character of the one is pitted against the chaotic yet creative temperament of the other.

Early in June 1920 Joyce for the first time met Ezra Pound, who found him 'stubborn as a mule or an Irishman' but not 'at all *unreasonable*' (Ellmann, *Joyce*, 480). On Pound's suggestion the Joyce family moved to Paris on 8 July, into a tiny flat close to the Bois de Boulogne. Without income, they lived on Pound's personal generosity. The world of Parisian letters began to make a place for Joyce: within three days of reaching the city, he had met Paul Valéry at the home of Natalie Clifford Barney. In John Rodker he found a genial admirer who became the nominal publisher of the Egoist edition of *Ulysses*. On 11 June, at the home of André Spire, Joyce was introduced to Sylvia Beach, proprietor of Shakespeare & Co., who became his most important supporter after Miss Weaver. In August he met T. S. Eliot and Wyndham Lewis at the Hôtel Élysée, Eliot bearing a parcel of shoes from Pound to replace the tennis shoes that Joyce was reduced to wearing. This drove him to pick up the bill for an expensive meal while otherwise displaying what Eliot called 'punctilious reserve'.

Joyce soon, however, moved to a luxurious apartment at 5 boulevard Raspail using £200 supplied by Miss Weaver. (Her support did not fail in his lifetime and even extended to his family afterwards.) On Christmas eve Sylvia Beach arranged a meeting between Joyce and the influential critic and translator Valery Larbaud, who 'raved' about *Ulysses* and acted as its chief publicist in France, giving the book an immense impetus by means of a pre-launch lecture at La Maison des Amis des Livres on 7 December 1921. In the interim, however, the 'Nausicaa' episode became the object of a formal complaint by the Society for the Prevention of Vice in New York, and issues of the *Little Review* were confiscated and burnt by the US post office in September 1920, others having been previously sequestered in January and May 1919. In the hearing at the court of special sessions in February 1921, the editors of the magazine were fined $50 on the understanding that the lapse would not be repeated. Although the lawyer John Quinn believed that the entire book might be more easily defended than a single episode, Huebsch was sufficiently rattled to withdraw his undertaking to publish *Ulysses* in America.

Joyce's despondency at these events led Sylvia Beach to request 'the honour of bringing out your *Ulysses*' in Paris. It was agreed that an edition of 1000 copies would be produced using the Dijon printer Maurice Darantière. It was simultaneously agreed that the Egoist Press in London would buy the Darantière plates to publish a London edition as soon as the Paris imprint was sold out. Yet the book had still to be completed; and, though Joyce confidently predicted that he would finish writing it by the summer, iritis and other difficulties intervened in the months ahead.

Calamity struck when a Mr Harrison, employed in the British embassy, indignantly grabbed a portion of the 'Circe' episode of *Ulysses* from his wife, who was typing it from manuscript, and thrust it in the fire. John Quinn reluctantly repaired the loss with a photostat of the fair copy, which he purchased as Joyce produced it. Joyce's health now deteriorated dramatically. In July and again in August he lost consciousness, with fear of rats being the proximate cause, though drinking bouts stood behind each occasion. A serious attack of iritis prevented work for five weeks in July and August. Robert McAlmon, who with Djuna Barnes and Wyndham Lewis was a drinking companion, provided Joyce with a monthly stipend of $150 throughout 1921 and assisted with some typing. Another boon companion was Arthur Power, the Irish painter whom Joyce met in Montparnasse and who carefully recorded their conversations for posterity. A visit from Con Leventhal, who later introduced Samuel Beckett to him, soon resulted in the sole enthusiastic notice that *Ulysses* received in Dublin in his lifetime.

From June to October 1921 Joyce worked on the galley sheets from Darantière, embarking on the habit of marginal revision that characterizes so much of the textual history of *Ulysses*. In places he added one-third as much again to the margins, poring over his notebooks for additional material. With 'Penelope' and 'Ithaca' finished in October, and the passages omitted by *The Egoist*'s printer all reinstated, *Ulysses* was published on 2 February 1922. It was Joyce's fortieth birthday, and Sylvia Beach gave one copy, in its distinctive cobalt blue covers with white lettering (chosen after the Greek flag), to Joyce. Though it was promised to Miss Weaver, Joyce inscribed his copy to Nora, who never read it. As a result of Larbaud's advocacy, the subscription list for the first edition is a veritable almanac of leading French and English authors, though André Gide and George Bernard Shaw pointedly abstained. On 16 June 1922 Joyce celebrated the first 'Bloomsday', as the day on which the action of *Ulysses* occurs was known from that time, and on 12 October the Egoist edition was published in London. Within four days the agreed print run of 2000 was fully subscribed, although problems with delivery resulted in some copies being smuggled across borders. Confiscations accounted for some 400–500 copies in America, while the British customs seized 499 at Folkestone shortly after a further run of 500 had been printed in 23 January to make up for the American losses.

'Work in Progress'

A history of the world

In 1922 and 1923 Joyce's health was again pre-
carious. While Nora was in Ireland, following a
period of domestic tension, he suffered an acute
attack of iritis late in May 1922 and a physician
observed him living in considerable squalor at
rue de l'Université. On an endocrinologist's recommendation all his teeth were extracted, and
shortly afterwards he underwent a sphincterec-
tomy on his left eye. But meanwhile Joyce showed
signs of bestirring himself in new writing. To
Miss Weaver he had said that he was thinking
of composing 'a history of the world' (Ellmann,
Joyce, 537)—the first intimation of the ground
plan of *Finnegans Wake*. In February 1923 he
sorted out 12 kilograms of notes for *Ulysses*, and he
began about this time a notebook later published

as *Scribbledehobble*, which consisted largely of unused material from earlier works under headings based on the *Dubliners* stories. It was the first of nearly seventy such notebooks which went towards the making of *Finnegans Wake*. Though Joyce may have shown Larbaud a very early draft of the 'Tristan and Isolde' passage of the *Wake* in March 1922, it was not until 10 March 1923 that he made a formal start in sketching the 'King Roderick O'Conor' episode—the so-called first fragment of *Finnegans Wake*—writing to Miss Weaver, 'the leopard cannot change his spots' (*Letters*, 1.202). Joyce's benefactor soon demonstrated her commitment to his genius—to be tested hard in the ensuing seventeen years—by settling a further £12,000 on Joyce. After 'St Kevin' and 'The Colloquy of St Patrick and the Druid' swiftly followed, he produced 'Mamalujo' (*Finnegans Wake*, 2.4) as a framing chapter for the revised version of 'Tristan and Isolde'. Six of the eight sections of book 1 were written consecutively during 1923, with sections 1 and 4 being added in 1926–7. (An earlier draft-writing than all of these, written in the hand of Nora Joyce, was discovered among six manuscript sheets recently acquired by the National Library of Ireland, but its genetic relation to the whole has yet to be determined.)

Ford Madox Ford offered to publish part of 'Work in Progress'—as Ford dubbed it—in *transatlantic review*, where a draft of 'Tristan and Isolde' appeared as a 'literary supplement' in April 1924. In November T. S. Eliot's essay '*Ulysses*, order, and myth' appeared in *The Dial* (1923), announcing that the 'mythic order' of Joyce's *Ulysses* had 'the importance of a scientific discovery'—a distinct compensation for the fact that Eliot had been unwilling to review *Ulysses* when it appeared. Joyce, meanwhile, was determined to sustain his reputation as an author adept at more conventional forms of literature and permitted five poems from *Chamber Music* to appear in the Frankfurt magazine *Der Querschnitt* (1923). Shakespeare & Co. reprinted *Ulysses* in the first unlimited edition in the new year, incorporating a list of corrections which had been supplied by Joyce himself but which were not applied to the text until the reset Bodley Head edition of 1960. On 7 March 1924 he sent 'Anna Livia Plurabelle' to Miss Weaver, with a letter explaining its narrative framework: 'a chattering dialogue across the river [Liffey] by two washerwomen who as night falls become a tree and a stone' (*Letters*, 1.213). Joyce had completed 'Shaun the Post' by late May and composed the moving poem 'A Prayer!', expressing the masochistic but not abject relation to Nora from which much of his energy as a writer may have proceeded: 'Blind me with your dark nearness … beloved enemy of my will!'

Recurrent health problems did not prevent Joyce's carrying 'Work in Progress' forward dramatically during 1925. A four-page section on 'the Earwickers of Sidlesham in the Hundred of Manhood' (1.2) appeared in McAlmon's *Contact Collection of Contemporary Writers* in May, while a sample of the 'Mamafesta' chapter (1.5) was published in Eliot's *Criterion* in July 1925. Anna Livia Plurabelle (1.8) made her first appearance in *Navire d'Argent* (1 October 1925), and Ernest Walsh published a draft of the 'Shem' chapter (1.7) in *This Quarter* (1925–6). Early in June the Joyces moved to 2 square Robiac, off rue de Grenelle, where they remained until 1931; this was their most lasting residence in Paris. By November Joyce was near the end of 'Fourth Watch of Shaun' (bk 3). In February 1926 the first English-language production of his play *Exiles* was staged at the Neighbourhood Playhouse in New York, followed in the same month by a London première by the Stage Society, after an inordinately long delay, which elicited praise from Bernard Shaw.

The writing of book 2 and emendations to other sections occupied Joyce from 1926 to 1938, but he was preoccupied with eye trouble (he worked with a magnifying glass), the mental illness of his daughter Lucia, and the growing alienation of supporters. No new sections of 'Work in Progress' were published during 1926. For much of the year Joyce was busy revising the 'Mime of Mick, Nick and the Maggies' and the other three chapters of book 2. Besides that he produced the new episodes 'Triangle'—later part of 'Night Lessons' (2.2)— and the opening pages of *Finnegans Wake*. About this time Ezra Pound stated that 'nothing short of divine vision or a new cure for the clapp' could be worth 'all that circumambient peripherisation' (Read, 228).

In summer 1927 Joyce wrote the 'Questions' section of 'Work in Progress' (1.6). Between April and November, Eugene and Maria Jolas, Joyce's greatest literary allies in advancement of 'Work in Progress', published the first eight sections in *transition*, their 'international quarterly for creative experiment', resuming again in 1928 and 1929 with 'Night Lessons' and 'Four Watches of Shaun'. The Jolases adopted the work as the icon of their 'revolution of the word', a 'mantic' conception of language which, since free from any positive metaphysics, proved easier to combine with Freudianism, surrealism, and ultimately post-structuralism than with religion or theosophy, which proved convenient to contemporaries, and even more so to later Joycean commentators. With a definite literary forum, Joyce secured the support of Stuart and Moune Gilbert (Stuart Gilbert helped with the French translation of *Ulysses* in 1929, and in 1930 wrote a study of *Ulysses* based on Joyce's information), Paul and Lucie Léon, Louis Gillet, Nino Frank, and Samuel Beckett, while older friends dropped away. One such was Wyndham Lewis, who in the autumn of 1927 published in *Time and Western Man* an unflattering 'analysis of the mind of James Joyce', whom he accused of introducing a 'suffocating, neotic expanse of objects, all of them lifeless' into his work. Joyce retaliated in a scathing portrait of Lewis as an antisemitic, pro-fascist woman-hater in 'The Mookse and the Gripes' and the fable 'The Ondt and the Gracehoper' (3.1).

Crisis and consolidation

By September 1928, having returned to Paris from a trip to Salzburg, Frankfurt, Munich, and Le

Havre, Joyce found his eyes deteriorating to an extent that virtually prevented him from working in 1931. A hostile review from Seán O'Faoláin in *Criterion* in the autumn upset him greatly, especially as he feared that T. S. Eliot was also turning against him. In October 1928 *Anna Livia Plurabelle* came out as a pamphlet in New York. Meanwhile, Joyce had organized the compilation of a book that appeared in May 1929 under the title *Our Exagmination round his Factification for Incamination of Work in Progress* with essays from Beckett, Gilbert, Frank Budgen, Robert McAlmon, Thomas MacGreevy, Marcel Brion, Victor Llona, Elliot Paul, John Rodker, Robert Sage, and William Carlos Williams, as well as letters of protest from G. V. L. Slingsby and Vladimir Dixon—the latter an illiterate correspondent long thought to be Joyce, but in fact real. In August the Black Sun Press in Paris issued *Tales Told of Shem and Shaun*, comprising 'The Mookse and the Gripes', 'The Muddest Thick that was Ever Heard Dump', and 'The Ondt and the Gracehoper', with a foreword by C. K. Ogden and a 'symbol' of Joyce's 'sens du pousser' by Brancusi, which caused John Stanislaus Joyce to remark that 'the boy seems to have changed a good deal' (Ellmann, *Joyce*, 614).

In England during summer 1929 Joyce met Eliot to discuss the forthcoming publication of *Anna Livia Plurabelle* (1930), and made a recording from it at the BBC in what Harold Nicolson later called his 'Anna Livia voice' (Hutchins, 176). Joyce, who had for some time thought he might hand over *Finnegans Wake* to another writer, visited James Stephens, who offered to complete it if his eyesight should fail. The appearance of 'Fourth Watch of Shaun' in *transition* in November 1929 marked a change of tempo for Joyce, since financial problems obliged the Jolases to discontinue publication until 1933. Henry Babou and Jack Kahane brought out *Haveth Childers Everywhere* in Paris and New York; this was the only fragment to be published in 1930 (Faber issued it in 1931). Further eye operations in Zürich markedly improved Joyce's sight. His suspicions about psychoanalysis were confirmed when Jung wrote a foreword for the third German edition of *Ulysses* that was both irrelevant and offensive. Jung subsequently mollified Joyce, calling the 'Penelope' chapter a 'non-stop run of psychological peaches' (ibid., 182). (This was some mild compensation for the fact that Sigmund Freud had independently declared that, of all the races, the Irish alone were immune to psychoanalysis.) In December he found a willing hagiographer, Herbert Gorman (*James Joyce* was not published until 1939), and himself worked on the French translation of *Anna Livia Plurabelle* started by Samuel Beckett and Alfred Péron (it was completed by Paul Léon, Eugene Jolas, and Ivan Goll).

In 1931 Sylvia Beach accepted the *Ulysses* manuscripts in lieu of world rights, and the novel was brought out in America by Random House in 1934 having been judged 'honest' and 'sincere' by a United States district court judge. Albatross Press took over publication of the novel in Europe, issuing the Odyssey Edition of 1932, which was seen through the press by Stuart Gilbert. (An English edition published by John Lane appeared in 1936.) In 1931 Joyce also signed a contract for the English edition of *Finnegans Wake* with Faber and with B. W. Huebsch at New York's Viking Press.

On 4 July 1931 Joyce and Nora were married, 'for testamentary reasons', at Kensington register office, Joyce singing 'Phil the Fluther's Ball' and 'Shule Aroon' in celebrations afterwards at Robert Lynd's home at 5 Keats Grove. The date, intentionally, was Joyce's father's birthday. At the end of the year, on 29 December, John Stanislaus Joyce died. Surprisingly, the old man left an estate of £665 0s. 9d. gross, of which £36 12s. 1d. remained to Joyce, the sole beneficiary, after debts were paid. Joyce experienced 'self-accusation' and 'prostration of mind', but this was alleviated when Giorgio (now George) and his wife Helen Fleischman, whom he had married in December 1930, provided him with a grandson, Stephen, on 15 February 1932. Joyce marked the occasion with the poem 'Ecce puer', which contained the lines:

> Young life is breathed
> On the glass
> The world that was not
> Comes to pass ...
> O, father forsaken,
> Forgive your son!

Lucia's troubling behaviour at this period reached a crisis on Joyce's fiftieth birthday, when she threw a chair at her mother and was removed by George to a *maison de santé*: this was her first entry into medical care. Her unrequited love for Samuel Beckett, and a disastrous engagement to Alex Ponisovsky, who had taught Joyce Russian, had added to her distress, and she was diagnosed—possibly mistakenly—with hebephrenia, an incipient form of schizophrenia. Joyce was racked with anxiety and guilt about his daughter ('Whatever spark of gift I possess has been transmitted to Lucia, and has kindled a fire in her brain'; Ellmann, *Joyce*, 650), and arranged for her to design 'lettrines' for *A Chaucer ABC* (1936). With his right eye virtually beyond repair, he worked on through the autumn with the children's chapter of 'Work in Progress' (2.1). The mordant humour of its celebrated conclusion—'Loud, heap miseries upon us yet entwine our arts with laughters low'— triumphantly reflects its author's state of mind at that period. (It was issued by the Servire Press in June 1934 with designs by Lucia.) *Two Tales of Shem and Shaun* was also published as a pamphlet in 1932.

In 1933 Joyce suffered from colitis, an indication of the illness that eventually killed him, but the news of the American edition of *Ulysses* inspired some jubilation. With his daughter in a sanatorium early in 1934, Joyce worked 'every day alone at my big long wide high deep dense prosework' (Ellmann, *Joyce*, 673). But on 15 September Lucia, now also suffering from leucocytosis, set fire to her room and was transferred to Zürich Mental Asylum before being moved to a private sanatorium at Küsnacht where Jung was a consultant.

Despite Joyce's misgivings about Jung as a critic he thought he might be able to help his daughter. Indeed for a time Lucia responded well to Jung and Joyce was reassured. When Jung suggested that Lucia was her father's *anima inspiratrix*, Joyce removed her in January 1935. He later told Jung that he and his daughter were both innovating a new literature. Jung believed however that they 'were like two people going to the bottom of a river', but Lucia was drowning while her father was diving (Ellmann, *Joyce*, 679). Meanwhile Lucia was temporarily put in the care of her aunt Eileen in Bray and Miss Weaver in London, who were tested to the limit. Joyce himself was melancholic, doubting if 'anything lies ahead of us except ruin' (*Letters*, 3.332), as he wrote to Budgen.

Throughout this period Joyce strenuously resisted the idea that Lucia was mad or that her fixation on him was anything more than the hypersensitivity of an affectionate daughter for whose disordered state of mind he felt immense responsibility and a profound compassion. His letters to Miss Weaver mingled anger and scepticism at the disturbing information given him, while she, attempting to obey his injunction that Lucia be spoken of as normal, understated the extremity of her behaviour. Late in 1935 Lucia was removed in a straitjacket from an establishment at Neuilly after further violent behaviour, and was threatened with incarceration in a state asylum. Joyce, now recognizing that she was in 'the abyss of insanity', was able to have her transferred to a *hôtel de santé* at Ivry-sur-Seine, where she remained until 1951. (She was then moved to St Andrew's Hospital, Northampton, where she remained until her death in 1982.)

With Lucia safe at Ivry—where he visited her each week—Joyce, notwithstanding attacks of colitis and the usual financial troubles, was more relaxed than for some years previously, expressing himself on life and literature with uncharacteristic freedom to friends and visitors. He spent much time in 1937 conferring with Nino Frank about the Italian translation of *Anna Livia Plurabelle*, and Samuel Beckett was also in his company. *Storiella as She is Syung* was published by the Corvinus Press in London in October 1937, containing passages from 'Night Lessons'. 'Work in Progress' was drawing to conclusion with galley proofs, page proofs, and the last manuscript pages of book 4 keeping Joyce occupied for sixteen hours a day, by his own estimation. In Zürich in late summer 1938 Joyce ignored advice to undergo examination after severe stomach cramps, and returned to Paris as war loomed. Joyce barked at Stanislaus: 'Don't talk to me of politics, all I am interested in is style.' His indifference did not prevent his helping Herman Broch to reach England in March 1938, nor, as Bernard McGinley points out, his involvement with Giuseppe Bertelli in trying to help Jewish refugees to get to America. But his unwillingness to protest against Nazism in print disappointed several friends.

In the fraught atmosphere after the Munich pact, the last passage of 'Work in Progress', or *Finnegans Wake*, as it was now to be known, was composed, ending on 13 November 1938 with the inscription 'un rien, l'article the'. Joyce's sense of pride and relief was such that, for some days afterwards, he carried the manuscript with him. Joyce had hoped to publish *Finnegans Wake* on his father's birthday in 1938, but instead one unbound copy reached him on 30 January 1939. Faber in London and the Viking Press in New York simultaneously published his final work on 4 May 1939.

Finnegans Wake

'That source itself'

The most conspicuous innovation of *Finnegans Wake* is its use of 'dream-language'. After *Ulysses* Joyce believed that he had 'come to the end of English', and his last novel is a pervasive layering of multilingual puns in successive drafts which produces a fabric rich in semantic possibilities but almost impenetrable to the general reader. Joyce's method is demonstrably modern, having more to do with philology and psychoanalysis than with symbolism and magic, but it is none the less informed by a sacral relation to language as a kind of 'broken heaventalk' in which truth subsists in a dismembered way. He was unorthodox in his beliefs but he used the terms 'soul' and 'spirit' passionately, and he did not accept the premises of a vacuous form of relativism. *Finnegans Wake* is patently the most relativistic of all literary texts, yet it is also the most absolute in that it attempts to reconstruct 'the reality of experience' through a vast system of correspondences. If developed to the uttermost, these produce a representation of humanity whose claim to truth is its completeness as a 'selfbounded and selfcontained' entity whose 'soul' 'leaps from the vestment of its being'. In order to effect this Joyce made H. C. Earwicker, a publican in Chapelizod, co. Dublin, and reincarnation of Finn MacCool, the 'dreaming subject'. Like the Joyces, who spoke Triestino Italian at home, the Earwicker family is multilingual. No one language dominates in *Finnegans Wake*, except Hiberno-English, which has a comic vibrancy and lyricism. The characters occupy different times and places in the same (or opposite) person. The question 'Who is dreaming *Finnegans Wake*?' is not ultimately rewarding, yet it does point to the fundamental innovation, which is to let language itself constitute the reality of experience.

The relationship between the various textual stages of *Finnegans Wake* is even more anomalous than is the case with *Ulysses*. There was no fair copy, and multiple versions exist in notebooks, drafts, typescripts, and corrected proofs (now held at the British Library and the State University of New York at Buffalo). Moreover, many of the episodes were published in magazines and pamphlets, often not in their final state. *Finnegans Wake* therefore seems less like a book '*about* something; *it is that something itself*', as Samuel Beckett wrote of it (Beckett and others, 14). In one respect the final text of *Finnegans Wake* is, however, stable.

The title of the book—which was kept secret until 1938—was taken from an Irish-American ballad, a party piece in the Joyce household in Dublin, about Tim Finnegan, a drunken bricklayer who falls to his death from a ladder but returns to life when accidentally splashed with whiskey at his wake. Around this song, with its suggestion of reincarnation and eternal return, Joyce constructed a vast edifice of corresponding myths and narratives. Some of these were hallmark Irish and Judaeo-Christian, but other sources, including the Egyptian Book of the Dead and the comic-strip banter of Mutt and Jeff, provide an astonishing symphony of human voices to construct a universal history. Joyce's chief inspiration is Giambattista Vico, who divided human history into divine, heroic, and human ages followed by a *ricorso* (or return), setting the whole cycle in motion once again. In *Finnegans Wake* these ages correspond to the four books which constitute the whole work, as well as internal cycles within them. At the same time the *Wake* is structured by the idea of interdependent and mutually generating opposites which Joyce derived from Giordano Bruno and Samuel Taylor Coleridge, who wrote: 'Every power in nature or in spirit must evolve an opposite as the sole condition and means of its manifestation; and every opposition is, therefore, a tendency to reunion' (*Critical Writings*, 134).

Joyce's central 'characters' represent human life in a more comprehensive way than literary realism—and naturalism in particular—admits. They are archetypal while being located in a dense matrix of disparate and even contradictory literary and historical allusions. At the centre stands Humphrey Chimpden Earwicker with his consort Anna Livia Plurabelle, respectively embodied by the Hill of Howth and the River Liffey. In the central 'Night Lessons' chapter, Joyce presents a chart of 'the whome of your eternal geomater' which doubles as a map of Ireland and a diagram of the dynamic and often hostile relations between genders and siblings and (more problematically) between fathers and their daughters. The events that befall the Earwicker family in the *Wake* primarily concern a sexual misdemeanour committed by Humphrey in Dublin's Phoenix Park. This involves two girls and three soldiers, who are counterparts of Issy on the one hand, and Shem and Shaun on the other. Just as Issy becomes her mother, so the boys become their father. Earwicker is a male principle who readily bifurcates into his warring sons, while Issy represents the sexually attractive principle through whom the sons are reattached to the source of life. It is through loss of innocence that these necessary processes in the chain of reproduction are effected—a *felix culpa*, or happy fall.

Joyce's universal history

By 21 May 1926 Joyce had been able to write, 'I have the book fairly well planned out in my head' (*Letters*, 1.241). He insisted that the labour of composition was like tunnelling through a mountain from two sides, implying a general symmetry between the four latter sections of book 1 and those of book 3. For instance, Anna's soliloquy at the end of book 1 ('Anna Livia Plurabelle') is balanced by Earwicker's soliloquy at the end of book 3 ('Haveth Childers Everywhere'). 'The Mookse and the Gripes' in book 1 is a companion piece to 'The Ondt and the Gracehoper' in book 3. The structure of the text is a 'simple equilibrium of two symmetrical half-arches supporting a keystone of greater complexity', as Roland McHugh has remarked (McHugh, 6)—the keystone being the barely penetrable chapters of book 2.

Book 1 concerns Earwicker's crime, betrayal, demise, and burial. The fifth section offers a palaeographer's account of Anna's letter and a pastiche of Sir Edward Sullivan's preface to the Book of Kells, which serves also as a caricature of *Finnegans Wake* itself. The sixth poses twelve conundrums of great ingenuity, including 'The Mookse and the Gripes'. In the next section Shaun offers a portrait of the artist in which Stephen Dedalus is disparaged as a 'supreme prig', and the *Wake* itself as an 'epical forged cheque', comprising 'once current puns, quashed quotatoes, messes of mottage'. The last section is a *tour de force* with its 'chattering dialogue' between two washerwomen across the Liffey, discoursing on the scandalous failings of Earwicker. The episode

ultimately included the names of more than 500
rivers.

The first half of book 2 concerns the children, initially engaged in a charade-cum-matinée performance and afterwards at their homework. The third section, set in the public house, features two more Joycean fables—'The Norwegian Captain' and 'How Buckley Shot the Russian General'. It also frames Joyce's response to the invention of television and the splitting of the atom (respectively 'the bairdboard bombardment screen' and 'the abnihilisation of the etym' by 'the first lord of Hurtreford'). In the last section of book 2, the story of Tristan and Isolde is retold by the four evangelists ('Mamalujo'), who hover above the lovers' boat in the form of seagulls, each connected with a different province, as their accents reveal. These voyeurs also represent the four masters (compilers of the seventeenth-century Irish *Annals*) and, as such, all important redactors of hot-blood conquests. The section ends with the tragical history of 'King Roderick O'Conor', last high king of Ireland, whose 'babel tower and beamer' are reduced to 'diversed tonguesed', signifying the cultural disorder of a colonized realm. This was long thought to have been the first episode of 'Work in Progress' to be written, though its claim to primacy has recently been questioned. It nevertheless reveals the centrality of cultural hybridity to *Finnegans Wake* and to our interpretation of it. The groundedness of this condition in Irish history was Joyce's point before it was adopted by the post-colonial critics.

Book 3 traces the passage of Shaun the Post 'backwards through the events already narrated' while 'rolling up the Liffey in a barrel', as Joyce told Miss Weaver (*Letters*, 1.214). The first section, containing 'The Ondt and the Gracehoper', is followed by 'Jaun', who preaches moral hypocrisy to Issy and falls ignominiously to earth from his 'soapbox', while Issy turns to the more romantically interesting Shem ('Coach me how to tumble, Jaime'). As 'Yawn' in the third section, the eponymous postman is stretched out at the hill of Uisneach, a druidic centre of ancient Ireland, and becomes a conduit for contesting Irish voices from St Patrick to Parnell until, at last, being revealed as Earwicker. (The final passage was published as *Haveth Childers Everywhere* in 1930.) In the fourth watch, Earwicker's children witness a 'culious epiphany' as their father, wakened in the

night, unsuccessfully attempts sexual intercourse
with his wife ('You never wet the tea!') .

After this, the lowest ebb, Joyce takes his universal history back to dawn with the 'Ricorso' (book 4), conceived as a stained-glass window through which the sun rises at the pagan equinox. St Patrick, in legend associated with that season, contends with the archdruid Balkelly, in whom Bishop Berkeley and Johannes Erigena are equally mixed. Pantheism gives way to monotheism when the missionary ignites the paschal fire, bringing in a new cycle, just as life begins again when 'dawn-fire' touches the 'tablestoane ath the centre of the great circle of the macroliths' at Tara (or, more exactly, Newgrange). In spite of these masculine enactments of the idea of rebirth, it requires Anna's soliloquy at the end to usher in the new cycle of birth, marriage, and death, as she does with her imperative call: 'Finn, again!'

Last years

When war was declared on 3 September 1939 Joyce and Nora were in Brittany awaiting Lucia. From late 1939 to early 1940 they were on the move, from La Chapelle with Maria Jolas to

Vichy. Joyce passed his time preparing corrections for *Finnegans Wake* with Paul Léon (or 'adding commas', as he told George Pelorson), and telling Homeric stories to his grandson Stephen. In Paris Léon rescued Joyce's papers and saved other possessions which an unpaid landlord had auctioned. He deposited them with Count O'Kelly, the Irish ambassador, on the understanding that they should be given to the National Library of Ireland if he did not return to collect them. Léon soon afterwards fell into the hands of the Gestapo, and was murdered by a concentration camp guard in April 1942.

The Joyces left France for Switzerland, and arrived in Zürich on 17 December 1940. From the Pension Delphin Joyce issued messages of thanks to those who had assisted him—Jacques Mercanton, who signed the deposition denying that he was Jewish (which had led to his initially being refused a Swiss visa); Edmund Brauchbar (a businessman who had been a student of Joyce's in 1915), who had deposited 20,000 francs in a Zürich bank for which Joyce's friend Paul Ruggiero still worked; Ruggiero himself, who galvanized a support group; and Armand Petitjean and Louis Gillet, who gained permission for the Joyces to leave France. In the afternoons he walked in the snow with Stephen, stopping on one occasion to buy him books on Greek mythology.

On 7 January 1941 Joyce sent his last written communication, a card with a list of useful names for Stanislaus, who had been forced to move to Florence. After Ruggiero's birthday dinner on 10 January he suffered acute abdominal pains—the 'cramps' that had been troubling him periodically for many years. When a dose of morphine proved inadequate he was carried on a stretcher to the Schwesterhaus vom Roten Kreuz, 'writhing like a fish' according to his grandson's memory of the event (Ellmann, *Joyce*, 741). An X-ray revealed a perforated duodenal ulcer, and an operation was performed on 12 January. Joyce woke from anaesthetic and appeared to be recovering but started losing strength on Sunday and was given blood transfusions. Before Nora and George were sent away by the medical staff, he asked for Nora to lie down beside him. At 1 a.m. he woke and asked for them before slipping into a coma.

James Joyce died at the Schwesterhaus vom Roten Kreuz at 2.15 a.m. on 13 January 1941, before his family could arrive. The sculptor Paul Speck was commissioned to make a death mask. Joyce was buried at Fluntern cemetery in Zürich on 15 January, Nora refusing Catholic rites. The expenses of the funeral were paid by Miss Weaver, who readdressed to Nora the sum of £250 she was preparing to send to him. At the graveside were the British minister Lord Derwent, who made an address, the poet Max Geilinger, Professor Heinrich Straumann, and Max Meilor, a tenor, who sang 'Addio terra, addio cielo' from Monteverdi's *Orfeo*. Lucia received the news of her father's death with all the marks of her condition and a curious echo of Joyce's theme in his last book, saying, 'What is he doing under the ground, that idiot? When will he decide to come out? He's watching us all the time' (Ellmann, *Joyce*, 743).

The young Joyce who had arrived at University College, Dublin, in 1899 was 'tall, slim, and elegant' with 'an erect yet loose carriage; an uptilted, long, narrow head, and a strong chin that jutted out arrogantly; firm, tight shut mouth; light-blue eyes [that] could stare with indignant wonder', as Con Curran remembered him from that time (Curran, 4). In later years he grew conspicuously slighter but always retained a dandified air which he enhanced by a cane and rings. His hair was severely swept back, and he wore broad felt hats in the fedora style. He had the 'stork's legs' that he attributed to Leopold Bloom, and on these he occasionally danced an Irish jig of his own invention—the celebrated 'spiderdance'. The thin lips, determined chin, and prominent forehead of the young artist produced in time a somewhat concave physiognomy in the ageing writer which, when surmounted by the thick lenses of his round spectacles that magnified the conspicuous effect of repeated surgery to his left eye, oddly anticipated the aspect of the death mask. For Louis Gillet it captured 'a double expression of Noli me tangere and Non serviam', yet displayed also 'a smile mischievous and somewhat waggish' on his 'ironic mouth' as if to say, 'where I am, you'll never catch me . . . I slip away, unseen, unknown' (Potts, 178). But Joyce is neither unseen nor unknown today. Indeed, no figure in twentieth-century literature represents the idea of the literary artist more completely than the great Shem, in whom so many extraordinary elements of passion, observation, rebellion, invention, tenacity, and incomparable literary ability were combined.

The world as word

The Joyce archive

In view of the uniquely complex development of James Joyce's literary texts in notebooks, manuscripts, and typescripts, along with the author's practice of composing extensively on the printers' galleys, the study and appreciation of his art calls for an exacting examination of the written and printed materials involved at every stage. Voluminous materials of this kind have been dispersed throughout libraries and collections in Ireland, Britain, and the USA. Many of Joyce's papers are now held at the Lockwood Memorial Library of the State University of New York at Buffalo, together with the Joyce family portraits. The manuscript of *Stephen Hero*, which was edited and introduced by Theodore Spencer in 1944 and revised by John J. Slocum and Herbert

Cahoon to incorporate some additional pages, is at Harvard. The fair-copy manuscript of *A Portrait of the Artist as a Young Man* was presented to the National Library of Ireland by Harriet Shaw Weaver, while a definitive edition of the novel based on it was published in America in 1964 (and in the United Kingdom in 1968). The *Ulysses* manuscript which Joyce sold to John Quinn after a triplicate typescript had been produced from it remains intact at the Rosenbach Museum and Library in Philadelphia. After her offer to permit the repatriation of her husband's body was turned down by the Irish government, Nora Joyce ensured that Miss Weaver would donate the manuscript of *Finnegans Wake* to the British Museum rather than to the National Library of Ireland. In order to make the sum of such materials available to scholars, notebooks, manuscripts, typescripts, and corrected galleys for all Joyce's work were published in black and white facsimile by the Garland Press of New York as *The James Joyce Archive* (1977–9). A colour facsimile edition of the *Finnegans Wake* notebooks at Buffalo is now in progress (ed. V. Deane, D. Ferrer, and G. Lernout, 2001–).

Joyce's essays, lectures, reviews, and some of the extant notebooks were edited by Ellsworth Mason and Richard Ellmann as *The Critical Writings of James Joyce* in 1959. The poetry collections with sundry shorter writings including the 1904 'Portrait' essay were collected by Ellmann and others as *Poems and Shorter Writings* in 1990, a further critical compilation being issued by Kevin Barry as *Occasional, Critical, and Political Writings* in 2000. J. C. C. Mays's edition of *Poems and 'Exiles'* (1992) is also notable. A volume of Joyce's letters was edited by Stuart Gilbert in 1957, with two further volumes and a *Selected Letters* appearing under the hand of Richard Ellmann respectively in 1966 and 1975. (Joyce's so-called 'black letters' to Nora of 1909 are printed in the latter only.) In 1984 the Garland Publishing Company issued a controversial 'Critical and Synoptic Edition' of *Ulysses*, edited by Hans Walter Gabler on the basis of a hypothetical 'genetic text' comprising variants in working manuscripts, typescripts, complete editions, and serial publications whether within the direct line of textual transmission or not. The validity of this method and the authenticity (or even accuracy) of the result has been widely disputed, and conservative readers still adhere to the corrected Odyssey Edition and its successors as bearing the imprimatur of the author. *Finnegans Wake* has never been reset, though Joyce's corrections (which Maria Jolas carried out of France during the Second World War) were applied to the Viking Press and Faber editions in the 1950s. (In all editions the pagination and font are identical to those in the 1939 editions and each other.)

In December 2000 a 'lost' typescript of the 'Circe' episode of *Ulysses* was purchased by the National Library of Ireland for $1.5 million at auction in New York. The papers rescued from the Joyces' flat in Paris in autumn 1941 were lodged in the National Library of Ireland, as agreed, and became available for inspection by scholars fifty years later. A further body of papers in the possession of Paul Léon (including the lost 'Paris notebook' of 1904) was acquired by the Irish government in 2001. Most sensationally of all, the 'Pola Notebook' (MS 36,639/A/2) containing early drafts of the author's so-called 'aesthetic theory' (variously elaborated in *Stephen Hero* and *A Portrait of the Artist*), along with six manuscript sheets from 'Work in Progress' were exhibited at the National Library of Ireland in 2006. In 1967 the first Annual James Joyce International Symposium was held in Dublin—an event that entered into local academic folklore. A James Joyce Centre was established at 35 North Great George's Street, Dublin, adjacent to Belvedere College, in the 1990s and a 'Bloomsday' centenary symposium in the same lineage was held in Dublin in June 2004, when it occupied a good deal of public consciousness for a week. Plaques already set in the pavement several years earlier mark the major points in Joyce's Ulyssean hero's itinerary through the modern city, and Joyce himself has featured on an Irish banknote designed by Robert Ballagh.

Critical heritage

James Joyce's standing as a major writer in world literature was established during his lifetime. After the Second World War his promise to 'keep the professors busy' was widely realized in American and British universities. The 'guide' to *Ulysses* which Joyce had himself provided through the books of Frank Budgen and Stuart Gilbert made that novel less offputting than it might otherwise have been for many readers. Thus heralded, *Ulysses* could be treated either as a modernist and experimental text offering a new vision of society and a new method of literary representation, or as a classical affirmation of the humanist

principles deemed to underlie all great literature. Hence, those among the first generation of
'Joyceans' who devoted themselves to the arcana
of the texts—symbol and motif, structure and
significance, mythic parallels, and psychoanalyt-
ical hypotheses—sat comfortably with those who
exalted Leopold Bloom as the modern Ulysses, 'an
all-round man' and 'a keyless competent citizen'.

Finnegans Wake was a more daunting challenge,
but the work of early exegetes made it clear
that, for all its complexity, it shared the same
world of literary and popular consciousness as its
readers. Archetypal readings dominated the early
reception of the book yet, like *Ulysses*, it seems
to require an immense amount of local knowl-
edge also. The gleaning of sufficient Irish background became a badge of honour for the rapidly
growing tribe of Joyceans, enabled by the com-
parative rarity of a philosemitic modernist. There
was a distinct element of cultural tourism in all of
this, given that the establishment which embraced
Joyce was predominantly protestant and Anglo-
American. Joyce's agnosticism was, of course, a
help. That his mind was 'Irish', 'Catholic', and
even 'medieval' thus seemed less important than
the fact that he conceived of the world of culture

as a huge jigsaw of interlocking pieces in which no one narrative, still less one national tradition or one religious dispensation, easily prevailed. In this way he came to represent a syncretic view of human culture that began to dominate the increasingly liberal and sceptical orthodoxy of Western democracies in the second half of the twentieth century.

By the 1960s Joyce's reputation stood at the apex of a pyramid of international renown, with modernism, humanism, and psychoanalysis at its intellectual foundations. With only the Soviet realists standing out against him, he was hailed as an intrinsically democratic writer in the climate of cold war cultural politics even though the actual contents of his works (and to a great extent their manner) were at odds with the prevailing ethos of Western society at many material points. Thus Joyce posthumously managed to become both the epitome and the antithesis of cultural conformism though all the while a writer centrally respected for the magnitude of his talent and the scale of his achievement.

In 1926 Mary Colum told Joyce that *Anna Livia Plurabelle* was 'outside of literature', to which he replied, 'it may be outside literature now, but its future is inside literature' (Colum and Colum, 130). That he was proved right illustrates the coincidence between his idiosyncratic form of innovation and an anti-conventional impulse at the heart of much critical thought in late twentieth-century culture. From the 1960s onwards the 'deconstruction' of bourgeois certainties in ethics and belief increasingly characterized intellectual life first in Europe and then in America. Joyce's affinity with the 'Revolution of the Word' made him an ideal literary talisman. It was as the battering-ram of post-structuralism that he first figured in the writings of Jacques Lacan and others, who discovered in 'la jouissance de Joyce' an image of their own rebellion against the fixity of language and meaning.

For an anti-authoritarian movement such as feminist studies, the connection between the political agenda and the texts themselves was intrinsically unstable. If *écriture féminine* is the currently accepted tag for Joyce's way of writing from 'Penelope' in *Ulysses* onwards, Molly Bloom was nevertheless the creation of an author who claimed not to hold intellectual women in high regard—though Mary Colum challenged the truth of this assertion when he made it in her presence At the same time Molly's sensuality, together with her amenability to mythopoeic treatment as a type of Gea-Tellus, ultimately contributes more to her role in the book than her mental agility in measuring men's real stature and the position of women relative of them. Certainly Joyce believed that women's liberation was the central revolution of the twentieth century (as he told Arthur Power), but if he valued their subjectivity and regarded union with them as a necessary measure for the creative imagination, it did not mean that he endowed them with a plenitude of artistic power in their own right.

The rise of post-colonial studies in the 1990s provided a more rewarding means of analysing Joyce's subversive attitude towards the dominant form of Anglophonic culture—an attitude readily ascribed to him by Anglo-Saxon contemporaries whether inside or beyond the avant-garde movement. The point was epitomized by H. G. Wells when he wrote to Joyce: 'while you were brought up under the delusion of political suppression I was brought up under the delusion of political responsibility.' The difference indicated here is national. On the question of style, Wells admitted his desire to keep 'language and statement as simple and clear as possible', hence implying that Joyce, to the contrary, was inspired by Fenian malice towards the well of English undefiled. Joyce offers some support for this by means of a counter-reformational thrust in *Finnegans Wake*, where he appears to describe the linguistic outcome of the book as 'One sovereign punned to petery pence'. In fact the differences instanced by Wells are very real. Where his ideal is 'a big unifying and concentrating process' resulting in a kind of '*progress* not inevitable but interesting and possible', Joyce dismisses progress as the self-aggrandizing fantasy of Shaun-types who exercise power through the abuse of language. It is clear today that Wells's talk of 'increase of power and range by economy and concentration of effort' (*Selected Letters*, 364–5) is the stuff of textbook imperialism, as his *History of the World*, for all its liberality, reveals on every page. From this standpoint, the difference in their outlooks is actually that between the colonizer and the colonized no less than that between Enlightenment and modernist epistemologies, or that between protestant and Catholic, as Wells openly concedes.

Joycean criticism began—like Joycean biography—with American scholars whose arrival in Ireland to investigate his formative conditions resembled an anthropological expedition. Richard Ellmann's biography saw Irish literary life in the wider context of Western literary values—as can be seen in how he glosses Joyce's great discovery in *Ulysses* in terms of the word 'love' in all its human ramifications. It is a view which sets Leopold Bloom—sceptical, kindly, ordinary, imaginative, human—against the nationalist 'citizen' of the 'Cyclops' chapter—an embodiment of prejudice, bitterness, and hatred of the Anglo-Saxon. Ellmann goes so far as to cite the Irish nationalists who fought for independence as exemplifying those traits in the Irish national character least like the liberal secularism that Bloom (and, by implication, Ellmann himself) embodies.

Joyce and Ireland

In this way teams were formed with Joyce and Anglo-America on one side and Irish separatists on the other. Not surprisingly, recent Irish criticism has been much concerned with repudiating Joyce's Bloomian pacificism (if it is such) while emphasizing the 'Fenian' sympathies of the novelist in his incidental writings. This allies them with the post-colonial critics everywhere who argue that colonial peoples can attain authentic self-representation only when they shed the chains of imperial hegemony and, if possible, the language which sustains it; it does not, unfortunately, consolidate their bond with James Joyce, the chief writer to emerge from Catholic–nationalist Ireland at any time in its history. While Joyce as an eccentric Irishman, or at least a writer of genius at a tangent to the main line of national development (if not indeed the colonial remainder), has obvious attractions, it is also possible to accord him a great measure of ethical sense and political precedence in the context of the European Union. In any case, some further thinking about the underlying issues of colonial, anti-colonial, and post-colonial thinking is in order before the convincing critical repatriation of James Joyce can be completed.

It is clear that, in spite of the desires of Irish separatists at any period, post-colonial cultures are generally forced to acknowledge their own hybridity, thereby ending up more like Bloom than like Michael Cusack. Equally, in modern Irish society, Bloom stands nearer to the consensual view than the Fenians of *Ulysses*. Joyce undoubtedly offered a difficult nettle for Irish nationalists to grasp if they wished to see the half-Jewish and half-Irish advertising agent with a foothold in at least three religious camps as the best kind of modern Irishman. More than that: he clearly meant to antagonize those whom he had accused of circulating 'the pap of racial hatred'. In this sense *Ulysses* bears the stamp of his own subtly rebarbative personality and inveterate resistance to the encroachments of religion, nationality, language, and family (in a germane sense).

Post-colonialism, properly conceived, suggests an open approach to Joyce that allows for the best response to the facts of text and context. Yet '-isms' are only limited guides to works as complex as this author's and the worlds that he inhabited in structure and significance. There is much in Joyce that eludes liberal humanist and poststructuralist ways of thinking while also giving sustenance for one or the other kind of reading. Joyce's 'medievalism', which critics have often put aside as an unfortunate relic of his Irish Catholic (and, more specifically, Jesuit) education, is a case in point. This consisted in the incessant effort to make the intensely relative facts of reality and consciousness correspond in some large symbolic way to a unified image of reality. In view of an evident lack of engagement with this impulse, truly 'Joycean' criticism has arguably never yet been attempted. If it is to be written, it must be grounded primarily in the context of Irish literary history and the Irish cultural experience.

It has often been said that Joyce's experimentalism placed him in the vanguard of anti-bourgeois thinking. Yet, if so, it also placed him in an anomalous yet fertile relation to contemporary Irish nationalism. Ironically, in the light of the divergent courses of James Joyce and the modern Irish nation, his art carries forward the cultural project of the revivalists *vis-à-vis* the English canon, and the values that it supposedly embodies, in a far more radical way than any of his Irish contemporaries in literature or in arms. Joyce effectually overcame that canon by appearing to ignore it. While individually admiring Daniel Defoe and numerous English classics, Joyce professed that he had 'nothing to learn' from the English novelists as a whole, and made Flaubert and Ibsen his primary models. This did not signify an allegiance to one or other continental tradition so much as a commitment to what he called in 1904 a 'process of mind as yet untabulated' ('A Portrait of the Artist', *James Joyce: Poems and Shorter Writings*, 211): that is, an imaginative activity which disintegrates norms and standards in its attention to the sheer 'whatness' of experience and language.

The post-colonial concept of hybridity perhaps suggests the most comprehensive explanation of his essentially provisional methods as the writer reflecting a political, cultural, and psychological reality which is radically unstable and which affords no easy foothold to the consensual style of the liberal conscience. Positioned on the periphery of a powerful cultural formation such as English national literature, Joyce was well placed to discover the endless fissuring of experience in its received versions and conventional forms. At the same time he disdained the essentially reactive idealism of his nationalist contemporaries as well as those who came after him in Ireland (Samuel Beckett being the great exception).

It was thus that Joyce differed from those Irish contemporaries who wrote the orthodoxy of the revival and especially its Irish-Ireland wing comprising the Gaelic League and Sinn Féin. Hence the double aspect of his literary character: on the one hand he stands as a conservative exponent of the idea of literary value in the face of national chauvinism; on the other he is more radical than any nationalist in dismembering the cultural hegemony upon which the colonial state is founded. That Joyce saw so deeply into the social, psychological, and linguistic nexus that constituted the greater and the lesser worlds into which he had been born was the measure of his intellect. That he constructed a literary universe which admits of benefaction, trespass, transcendence, abasement, individuality and community, and the dream of the world/word as an ultimately integral thing, is the measure of his humane art. That he conceived and executed an entirely new form of writing in which waking and dreaming minds throw up an integral vision of the world as word is the measure of his genius.

Sources

R. Ellmann, *James Joyce* (1959); new and rev. edn (1982) · *Letters of James Joyce*, vol. 1, ed. S. Gilbert (1957); new edn (1966) · *Letters of James Joyce*, vols. 2 and 3, ed. R. Ellmann (1966) · *Selected letters of James Joyce*, ed. R. Ellmann (1975) · F. Budgen, *James Joyce and the making of 'Ulysses'* (1934); repr. (1960) · C. P. Curran, *James Joyce remembered* (1968) · J. Joyce, *Ulysses* (1967) · J. Joyce, *'A Portrait of the Artist as a Young Man': the definitive edition*, ed. C. Anderson and R. Ellmann (1968) · J. Joyce, *Stephen Hero: part of the first draft of 'A Portrait of the Artist as a Young Man'*, ed. T. Spencer, J. J. Slocum, and H. Cahoon (1956); rev. (1977) · *The critical writings of James Joyce*, ed. E. Mason and R. Ellmann (1959) · *James Joyce: poems and shorter writings*, ed. R. Ellmann, A. Walton Litz, and J. Whittier-Ferguson (1990) · T. S. Eliot, 'Ulysses, order, and myth', *James Joyce: two decades of criticism*, ed. S. Givens (1948) · S. Beckett and others, *Our exagmination round his factification for incamination of work in progress* (1929) · S. Gilbert, *James Joyce's 'Ulysses'* (1930) · H. Gorman, *James Joyce* (1939) · H. Levin, *James Joyce* (1941) · *Pound / Joyce: the letters of Ezra Pound to James Joyce*, ed. F. Read (1967) · P. Colum and M. Colum, *Our friend James Joyce* (1958) · J. Campbell and H. Robinson, *A skeleton key to 'Finnegans Wake'* (1944) · R. McHugh, *The sigla of 'Finnegans Wake'* (1976) · R. M. Kain, *Fabulous voyager: James Joyce's 'Ulysses'* (1947) · H. Kenner, *Dublin's Joyce* (1955) · P. Hutchins, *James Joyce's world* (1957) · S. Joyce, *My brother's keeper* (1958) · S. Joyce, *The complete Dublin diary of*

Stanislaus Joyce (1971) · R. Ellmann, *'Ulysses' on the Liffey* (1972) · R. Ellmann, *The consciousness of Joyce* (1977) · R. Ellmann, *The identity of Yeats* (1954); pbk edn (1964) · J. Atherton, *The books at the wake: a study of literary allusions in James Joyce's 'Finnegans Wake'* (1959) · S. L. Goldberg, *The classical temper* (1961) · R. M. Adams, *Surface and symbol: the consistency of James Joyce's 'Ulysses'* (1962) · C. Hart, *Structure and motif in 'Finnegans Wake'* (1962) · A. Walton Litz, *The art of James Joyce* (1961) · M. C. Solomon, *Eternal geomater: the sexual universe of 'Finnegans Wake'* (1969) · R. H. Deming, ed., *James Joyce: the critical heritage*, 2 vols. (1970) · A. Power, *Conversations with James Joyce* (1974) · H. Cixous, *The exile of James Joyce* (1976) · M. Norris, *The decentred universe of 'Finnegans Wake'* (1976) · M. French, *The book as world* (1976) · J. Garvin, *James Joyce's disunited kingdom and the Irish dimension* (1976) · C. H. Peake, *James Joyce: the citizen and the artist* (1977) · M. Groden, *'Ulysses' in progress* (1977) · A. Glasheen, *A third census of 'Finnegans Wake'* (1977) · W. Potts, ed., *Portraits of the artist in exile: recollections of James Joyce by Europeans* (1979) · C. MacCabe, *James Joyce and the revolution of the word* (1978) · S. Brivic, *Joyce between Freud and Jung* (1980) · D. Hayman, *'Ulysses': the mechanics of meaning* (1982) · D. Attridge and D. Ferrier, eds., *Post-structuralist Joyce* (1984) · F. Senn, *Joyce's dislocations: essays on reading as translation* (1984) · B. K. Scott, *Joyce and feminism* (1984) · B. Benstock, *James Joyce* (1985) · R. Brown, *James Joyce and sexuality* (1985) · K. Lawrence, *The odyssey of style in 'Ulysses'* (1981) · J. Bishop, *Joyce's book of the dark* (1986) · V. Mahaffey, *Reauthorising Joyce* (1988) · S. Henke, *James Joyce and the politics of desire* (1990) · B. Arnold, *The scandal of 'Ulysses'* (1991) · D. Attridge, ed., *The Cambridge companion to James Joyce* (1990) · P. Myers, *The sounds of 'Finnegans Wake'* (1992) · M. Beja, *James Joyce: a literary life* (1992) · P. Costello, *James Joyce: the years of growth, 1882–1915* (1992) · J. Fairhall, *James Joyce and the question of history* (1993) · J. Valente, *James Joyce and the problem of justice: negotiating sexual and colonial difference* (1994) · T. C. Hofheinz, *Joyce and the invention of Irish history: 'Finnegans Wake' in context* (1995) · E. Nolan, *James Joyce and nationalism* (1995) · V. J. Cheng, *Joyce, race, and empire* (1995) · C. van Boheemen-Saaf, *Joyce, Derrida, Lacan and the trauma of history: reading, narrative and postcolonialism* (1999) · M. Keith Booker, *'Ulysses': capitalism* and colonialism (2000) · P. McGee, *Joyce beyond Marx: history and desire in 'Ulysses' and 'Finnegans Wake'* (2001) · M. Hodgart, *James Joyce: a student's guide* (1978) · J. McCourt, *The years of Bloom: James Joyce in Trieste, 1904–1920* (2000) · B. Maddox, *Nora: a biography of Nora Joyce* (1988); repr. (2000) · J. McCourt, *James Joyce: a passionate exile* (2000) · J. Lidderdale and M. Nicholson, *Dear Miss Weaver: Harriet Shaw Weaver, 1876–1961* (1970) · B. McGinley, *Joyce's lives: uses and abuses of the biografiend* (1996) · B. Bradley, *James Joyce's schooldays* (1982) · J. B. Lyons, *James Joyce and medicine* (1973) · C. Fahy, ed., *The James Joyce–Paul Léon papers in the National Library of Ireland: a catalogue* (1992)

Index

Enjoy biography? Explore more than 55,000 life stories in the Oxford Dictionary of National Biography

The biographies in the 'Very Interesting People' series derive from the *Oxford Dictionary of National Biography*—available in 60 print volumes and online.

To find out about the lives of more than 55,000 people who shaped all aspects of Britain's past worldwide, visit the *Oxford DNB* website at **www.oxforddnb.com**.

There's lots to discover ...

Read about remarkable people in all walks of life—not just the great and good, but those who left a mark, be they good, bad, or bizarre.

Browse through more than 10,000 portrait illustrations— the largest selection of national portraiture ever published.

Regular features on history in the news—with links to biographies—provide fascinating insights into topical events.

Get a life ... by email

Why not sign up to receive the free *Oxford DNB* 'Life of the Day' by email? Entertaining, informative, and topical biographies delivered direct to your inbox—a great way to start the day.

Find out more at www.oxforddnb.com

'An intellectual wonderland for all scholars and enthusiasts'

Tristram Hunt, *The Times*

The finest scholarship on the greatest people...

Many leading biographers and scholars have contributed articles on the most influential figures in British history: for example, Paul Addison on Winston Churchill, Patrick Collinson on Elizabeth I, Lyndall Gordon on Virginia Woolf, Christopher Ricks on Alfred Tennyson, Frank Barlow on Thomas Becket, Fiona MacCarthy on William Morris, Roy Jenkins on Harold Wilson.

'*Paul Addison's* Churchill *... is a miniature masterpiece.*'

Piers Brendon, *The Independent*

Every story fascinates...

The *Oxford DNB* contains stories of courage, malice, romance, dedication, ambition, and comedy, capturing the diversity and delights of human conduct. Discover the Irish bishop who was also an accomplished boomerang thrower, the historian who insisted on having 'Not Yours' inscribed on the inside of his hats, and the story of the philanthropist and friend of Dickens Angela Burdett-Coutts, who defied convention by proposing to the Duke of Wellington when he was seventy-seven and she was just thirty. He turned her down.

'*Every story fascinates. The new ODNB will enrich your life, and the national life.*'

Matthew Parris, *The Spectator*

www.oxforddnb.com

At 60,000 pages in 60 volumes, the *Oxford Dictionary of National Biography* is one of the largest single works ever printed in English.

The award-winning online edition of the *Oxford DNB* makes it easy to explore the dictionary with great speed and ease. It also provides regular updates of new lives and topical features.

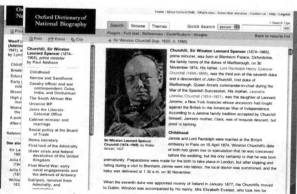

www.oxforddnb.com

The *Oxford Dictionary of National Biography* was created in partnership with the British Academy by scholars of international standing.

It was edited by the late Professor H. C. G. Matthew, Professor of Modern History, University of Oxford, and Professor Sir Brian Harrison, Professor of Modern History, University of Oxford, with the assistance of 14 consultant editors and 470 associate editors worldwide.

Dr Lawrence Goldman, Fellow and Tutor in Modern History, St Peter's College, Oxford, became editor in October 2004.

What readers say

'The *Oxford DNB* is a major work of reference, but it also contains some of the best gossip in the world.'

John Gross, *Sunday Telegraph*

'A fine genealogical research tool that allows you to explore family history, heredity, and even ethnic identity.'

Margaret Drabble, *Prospect*

'The huge website is superbly designed and easy to navigate. Who could ask for anything more?'

Humphrey Carpenter, *Sunday Times*

www.oxforddnb.com